handmade
JEWELLERY

ALISON RICHARDS

handmade JEWELLERY

techniques and design

PHAIDON

Phaidon Press Limited
Littlegate House, St Ebbe's Street, Oxford
First published 1976
© 1976 by Phaidon Press Limited

ISBN 0 7148 1698 1

Filmset and printed in Great Britain by
BAS Printers Limited, Wallop, Hampshire

Contents

Acknowledgments

The author and publishers wish to thank the following for their co-operation: the Crafts Advisory Committee; the Worshipful Company of Goldsmiths; Jones, Booty, and the Casson Gallery, all in London, for kindly lending pieces in their possession for photography, and Miss Susan Klimek who drew the illustrations.

Some of the processes described in this book are hazardous, involving danger from poisonous gases or burning. The publishers urge users to take the safety measures described. Although every effort has been made to ensure that the information given is accurate, no legal responsibility can be accepted for any errors or omissions, nor can the publishers or the author be held responsible for any loss or injury resulting from the use of this book.

1 Introduction

The interest in making jewellery has grown enormously in the last few years. Classes in Adult Education Institutes have multiplied dramatically, whilst applications to the Art School full time classes have increased. It is not hard to see why this should be. To make attractive jewellery, using for example silver and semi-precious stones, such as cornelian or garnets, is not difficult. The materials already have their own beauty; all one has to do is augment this by choosing the combination of materials and design. The satisfaction to be derived from making a piece of jewellery is enormous, whilst the costs are still relatively low.

Adult Institutes in Britain provide good facilities for learning to make jewellery as a pastime. Art schools provide courses for those who want to design and make jewellery at a professional level. Apprenticeship provides a third possibility for learning the skill and becoming a true craftsman. However, apprenticeships are not easy to come by, are poorly paid and traditionally last five years.

In this book, I have set out to give a detailed description of most of the techniques used in jewellery, an account of the tools needed and some suggestions and guidelines for design. My intention is that anyone enthusiastic enough would be able to teach him or herself to make jewellery with the aid of this book. But personal tuition is undoubtedly very valuable, so I also hope that it will be useful to students attending classes.

Becoming a really good craftsman takes practice and patience, but a thorough and systematic approach should produce good results from the beginning. In each chapter I have described how to make three or four pieces, starting with the simplest, and becoming progressively more complex. Do not feel too proud to copy existing work. The ideas I have suggested in the projects are designed to help you understand and become accustomed to the tools, the materials, and the processes. Of course they can be adapted or changed, but I hope that they may lead you to new ideas. If you find that you do not feel confident of your own design ideas, just try them out. You will find, I am sure, that once a piece is made or even begins to take shape, it will be enormously satisfactory. Even if it is not quite what you wanted or anticipated, it will give rise to new ideas and certainly more confidence. There is often the temptation initially to try to make much too complicated pieces, pieces which, for example, demand numerous delicate solder joints. When teaching, I find that new students often attempt to make things which even an experienced jeweller would not have attempted. Simplicity is very effective. The most successful and beautiful designs in every field of the arts are often the most simple; so although I don't want to quell any of your enthusiasm, I would warn against very ambitious ideas initially.

I hope that the following chapters will help you to master the enjoyment and rewards that jewellery making can bring.

2 Workshop and tools

The workshop

The space needed for a workshop is an area in any room big enough to accommodate the bench and with shelf space to house the polishing machine and other equipment. Good lighting is essential, natural light if possible. An adjustable lamp secured to the bench or screwed to the wall is necessary. The professional jeweller's bench is illustrated (**1**), but a solid table can be used. The unusual feature of a jeweller's bench is the semicircle cut from the topboard, which allows the jeweller to work more comfortably than at a straight bench. In the centre of the semicircular space, a wedge shaped piece of wood known as the 'pin' is bolted: this costs little or can be made easily. Nailed under the semicircle is a leather skin or thick sheet of plastic to catch the metal filings and off-cuts. A wire tool rack also nailed below the bench top is useful to keep the tools easily to hand. A wire coat hanger makes a good tool rack. The bench must be securely built and stand firm. The top should be at least $1\frac{1}{4}$in thick, and should not have any spring when struck with a hammer. Suggested measurements for the bench: height: 38in; width: 36in; depth: 27in; semicircle: diameter: 20in, radius 10in.

The polishing machine should be separate from the workbench, to avoid getting polish on the materials and equipment, and it should be bolted to a firm surface. A 3in engineer's vice bolted to the workbench or another secure surface is very useful. A filing cabinet with shallow drawers makes a good storage unit for tools and materials.

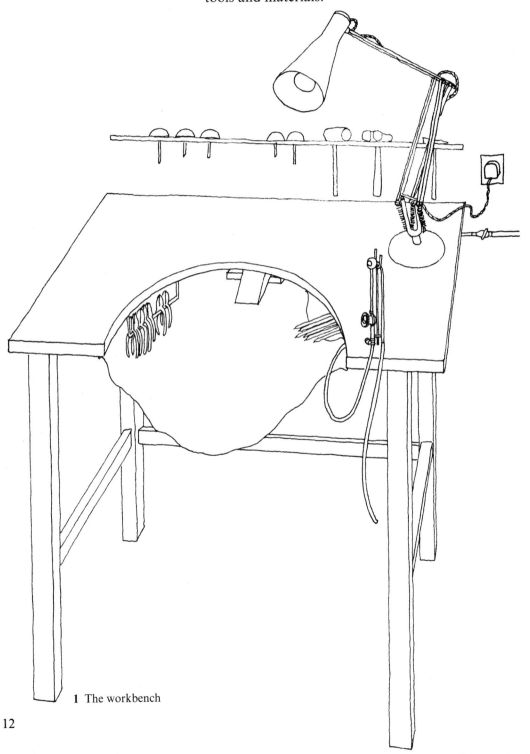

1 The workbench

The tools

The tools are grouped here according to usage, and not all of them are essential. A collection of hand tools to cover the requirements of the basic jewellery techniques may be acquired at a reasonable cost, tools for special purposes may be purchased when needed.

DRILLING AND CUTTING

Drills: either a hand drill with a selection of twist drills, or a drill stock/Archimedes drill with a selection of spade drills. A third possibility is a pendant drill, a luxury item but one which can also be used for various other processes, including polishing (**2**).

Jeweller's sawframe: 6in adjustable sawframe; the blade is held taut in the sawframe with a screw at either end of the frame (**3**).

Sawblades: sawblades in a variety of grades from coarse to very fine are available:
2/0 suitable for cutting BMG 18 (1·50mm) to BMG 8 (0·5mm)
00 for thicker material up to G.28 (3·15mm)
4/0 and 6/0 for very fine piercing work
A small magnet is useful for collecting broken sawblades.

Jeweller's top or side-cutting pliers: for cutting wire.

Files: a wide variety of files of different cuts is available. The measurements refer to the cutting length, not the total length (see **10**). The most necessary are:
6in flat file: Cut 6 (coarse cut for heavy work)
6in half round file or ring file: Cut 2 (for general use)
Needle files: at least nine shapes are available, but only four will be of great use – half round, round, triangular, barrette
Riffler files for filing otherwise inaccessible areas (**4**).

SHAPING AND BENDING

This is done with *pliers* (**6**).
Half round nose 4in or 5in: for curving metal
Flat nose pliers 4in or 5in: for holding and bending metal
Round nose pliers 4in: for making tiny rings and curves
Parallel pliers: for holding metal sheet or wire.
Of these the half round and the parallel are the most useful pliers.

Hand vices: the following implements facilitate handling small work (see **10**)

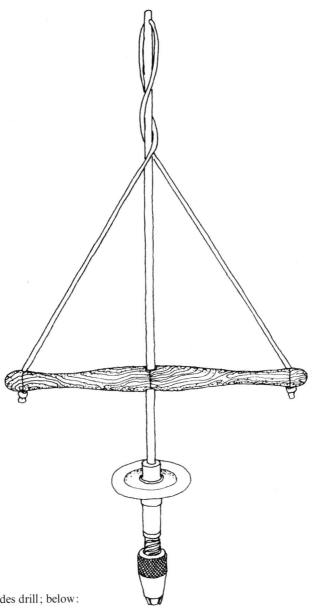

2, 3 Above: Archimedes drill; below:
adjustable piercing saw

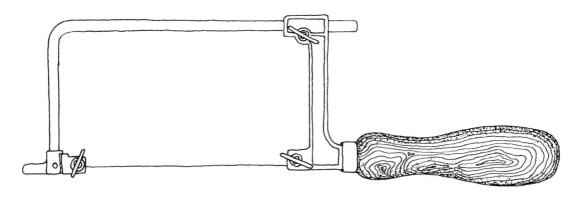

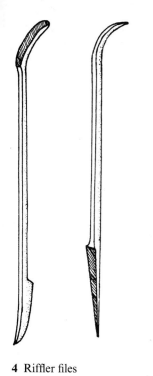

4 Riffler files

Pin vice: for holding wire and fine drills
Wooden ring vice: for holding rings when working on them or setting stones
Hand vice: for holding drills.

Draw plate: used for pulling wire down to a smaller wire gauge. It is a plate of hardened steel about $5 \times 1\frac{1}{2} \times \frac{1}{4}$in which has a series of twenty or thirty holes, graduated in size. They are obtainable in several different shapes, but round section, 1mm to 35mm, is the most useful.

Collet plate and punch: for trueing up collets into shape (**5**).

HAMMERING

Rawhide mallet or wooden mallet – diameter of head $1\frac{1}{2}$in: for flattening or shaping metal without marking or stretching it

Jeweller's hammer/riveting hammer – 2oz

Chasing hammer: especially balanced for chasing and repoussé work

Ballpein hammer: for use with punches and heavy work

Riveting or creasing hammer: for riveting and making chenier (**7**)

Flattening stake 3×3in: a hardened steel block providing a polished and flat surface, for flattening metal sheet. Any piece of hard steel with a flat surface may be used, eg an engraver's block.

Mandrel, triblet: a tapered steel rod for shaping and sizing rings (**8**)

Doming block and doming tools: a steel or brass block with hemispherical depressions of varying sizes for use with doming tools to make domes from flat sheet (**8**).

Steel rods of assorted diameters have two uses: they can be fashioned into punches by cutting or filing the ends, or used for making small rings. (Old drills and steel knitting needles can be easily adapted for these purposes.)

Lead block: is used for supporting metal when using punches. It can be made with lead scraps, eg piping, melted in an iron or aluminium saucepan and poured into a tin or wooden box, about 4×5in. Do not pour the dross, or skin, which forms on the molten lead.

CAUTION: Melt the lead in the open air or in a well ventilated room, as it gives off poisonous fumes when melting.

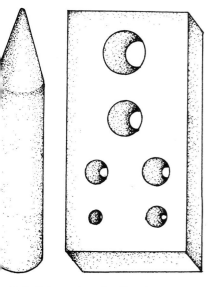

5 Collet punch and collet plate

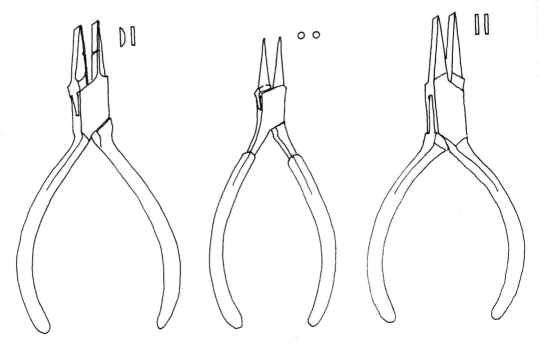

6 Above, left to right: half round
pliers; round nosed pliers; flat nosed
pliers
Below, left to right: side cutting pliers;
jeweller's shears or snips; parallel
pliers

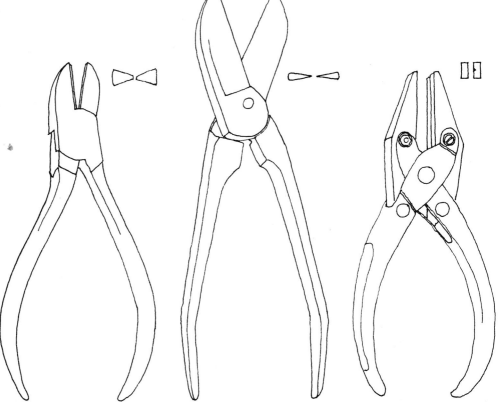

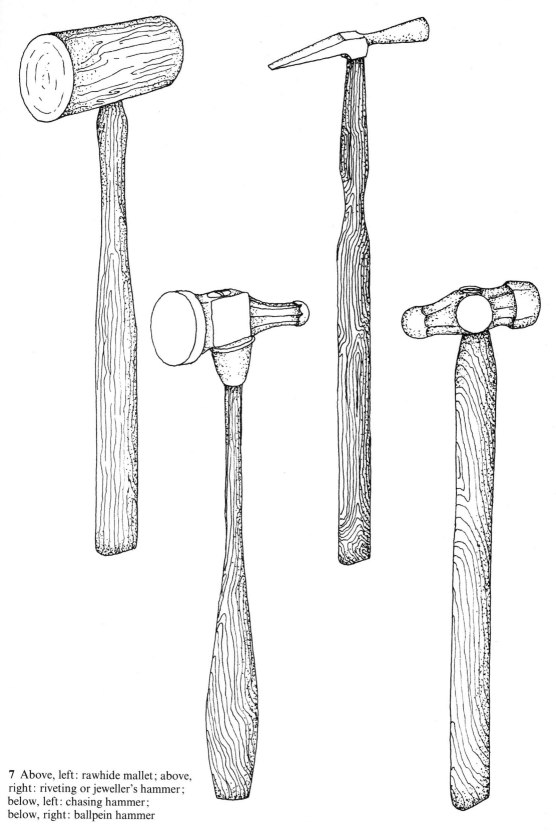

7 Above, left: rawhide mallet; above, right: riveting or jeweller's hammer; below, left: chasing hammer; below, right: ballpein hammer

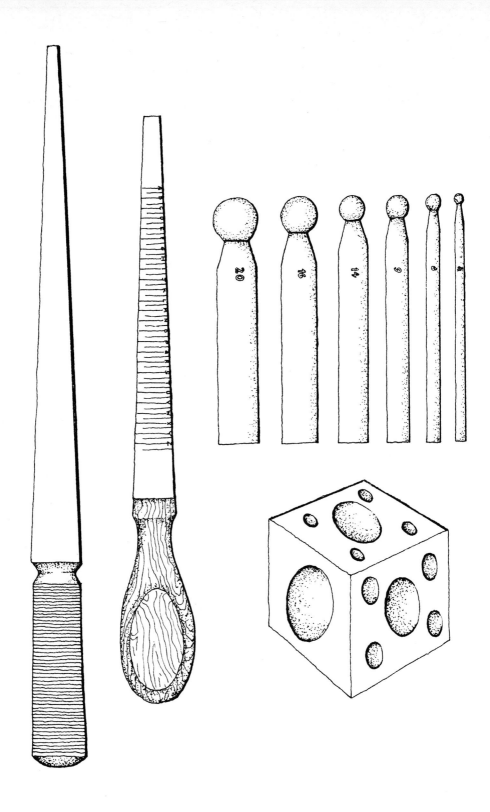

8 Left to right: triblet; ring size stick;
selection of doming punches;
below: doming block

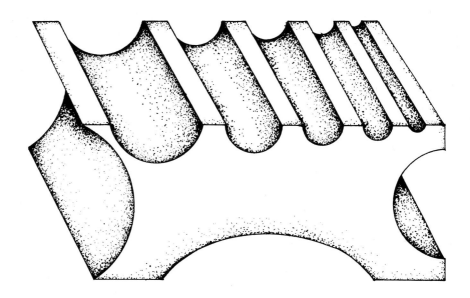

9 Swage block

Pitch block: is also used for supporting metal, for repoussé and chasing work. Traditionally an iron bowl with a rounded base is used to hold the pitch, but an enamel or aluminium bowl, about 6in diameter by 4in deep, half filled with lead to give weight and stability, or a shallow box such as a cigar box, is suitable. To make the pitch, heat 1lb Swedish pitch, but do not allow it to boil. When it is liquid, stir in about $\frac{1}{4}$lb powdered resin, then 1$\frac{1}{2}$lb plaster of Paris and lastly a lump of tallow the size of a large walnut. Pour this into the bowl or box you have selected.

Swage block: a steel block, the surface of which is cut with a series of grooves in a range of sizes for making chenier (**9**).

MEASURING

For this you will need (**10**):

Dividers: for measuring and marking out distances and circles

Metal rule, 6in or 12in long

Set square, 4in or 5in: for marking right angles and parallel lines

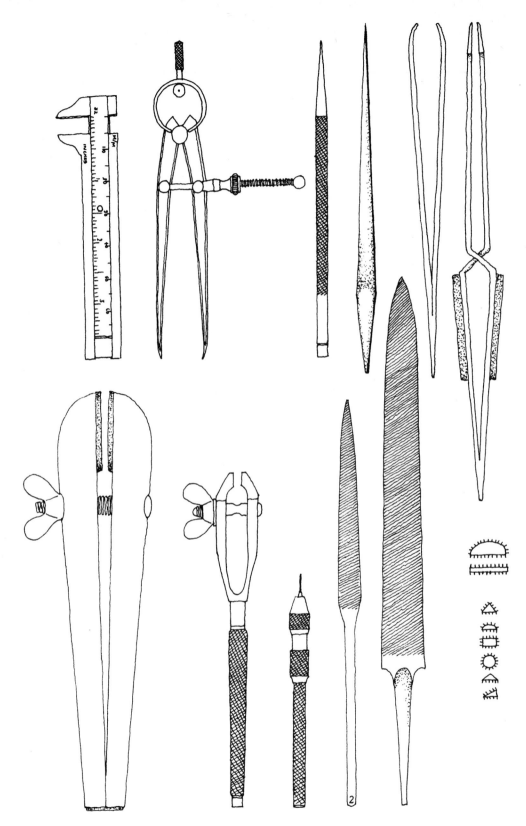

10 Above, left to right: measuring
slide; dividers; scriber; steel burnisher;
tweezers; soldering tweezers
Below: ring vice; hand vice; pin vice;
needle file; file; sections of files: top to
bottom: half round; flat; triangular;
half round; square; round; barrette;
knife

Brass measuring slide: for measuring thickness

Dixième gauge: for measuring $\frac{1}{10}$ of a millimetre. (This instrument is useful for the accurate measurement of wire or sheet metal thickness.)

SOLDERING

A variety of equipment is available for providing the heat necessary for soldering. If a mains gas supply is available near the workbench, it is probably the cheapest source of heat and is used with a mouth blowpipe. A tap should be fitted to the gas pipe near the workbench, and the supply connected to the blowpipe with a rubber tube. To the smaller tube opening on the blowpipe a second rubber tube and mouthpiece is fitted through which air is blown to direct the flame. Two separate blowpipes are available for use with natural gas and coal gas.

NOTE: Natural gas has not proved very satisfactory, due to the erratic pressure. The alternative is bottled butane or propane gas. A handpiece, a very fine nozzle and a length of connecting hose will be necessary.

Borax cone and unglazed earthenware dish: borax is used as a flux, mixed with water and ground to a thin paste on the dish. It is applied with a fine paint brush. Keep a small bottle of water to mix with the borax.

Asbestos sheet and charcoal block: a sheet of asbestos $6 \times 8 \times \frac{1}{4}$in is advisable on which to solder, and a charcoal block 3×4in on which to place articles to be soldered.

Cotter pins and iron binding wire G 30: to hold pieces in position for soldering.

Soldering tweezers: insulated with rubber handles to avoid burning the fingers when soldering.

Steel tweezers: for picking up small pieces and stones.

Copper or brass tweezers: for removing pieces from the pickle.

Pickle: the black skin of oxidation formed on metal by heating, is removed by acid. Either sulphuric acid or alum is used. Sulphuric acid must be diluted in the ratio one part acid to ten parts water, and kept in a glass or china container. It may be used cold, but is effective more quickly if heated, not boiled, in a copper pan.

CAUTION: Always add acid to water, not water to acid. If the acid comes into contact with the skin or clothes, it should be washed off immediately with water. Keep a supply of bicarbonate of soda to neutralize the acid.

Do not heat the acid in an unventilated room, as it gives off poisonous fumes.

Alum crystals dissolved in hot water provide a less hazardous alternative to sulphuric acid. The alum should be kept hot in a pyrex dish on an electric or gas ring. The alum is diluted in the ratio three tablespoons to one pint, and is obtainable from most chemists.

Use copper or brass tweezers to remove articles from the pickle, never use iron or steel, as these make the pickle discolour metals subsequently dipped.

FINISHING AND POLISHING

A selection of *emery paper* in three grades – 2/0 Fine, 00 General Use, 3 Coarse. An emery stick, a flat stick roughly $12 \times 1 \times \frac{1}{4}$in, round which the emery paper is wrapped tightly.

Water of Ayr stone (sometimes known as Scotch stone): soft grey stone in square section sticks, $\frac{1}{8}$in and $\frac{1}{4}$in. Used with water to rub away scratches in metal.

Burnisher of steel or agate

Polishing machine: polishing by hand produces a fine result but it is very time-consuming, so it is worth investing in a small polishing motor. A $\frac{1}{4}$-horse power motor will suffice. It should be bolted to a solid shelf or bench and separated from the normal working area. An electric drill held in an engineer's vice may be adapted with the addition of a tapered spindle or a flexible shaft. A variety of mops to be used on the polishing motor are needed:

$2 \times \frac{1}{2}$in felt lathe wheel – for polishing flat and plain surfaces
$2 \times \frac{1}{2}$in bristle lathe wheel – for general purposes
8 row bristle lathe end brush – for getting at difficult places
2 felt lathe fingers – for polishing the inside of rings
$1\frac{1}{2}$in fine bristle brush
$2 \times \frac{1}{2}$in calico mop
$2 \times \frac{1}{2}$in swansdown cotton mop

Polishing wheels for the pendant drill. These are useful for fine work. They can be used on the polishing motor with a plastic adapter which screws on to the spindle, or a flexible shaft which can be fitted to most polishing motors.

Bristle brush
Bristle end brush
$\frac{1}{8}$in felt wheel
Lambswool mop

With the polishing mops and brushes, use tripoli or pink porthos polishing compound, and finish with jeweller's rouge. Brass brushes and end brushes are also available. They can be used to give a matt finish.

STONE SETTING

A piece of $\frac{3}{16}$in square copper wire driven into a small handle obtainable from jewellers' suppliers, makes a useful pusher for setting stones.

Setting cement – for securing the piece to be set.

Methylated spirits – for dissolving the setting cement.

Pendant drill: both the polishing motor and the electric pendant drill are expensive items of equipment but both are extremely useful. The pendant drill is used for drilling, sanding and polishing small pieces, so if you are not inclined to make pieces with large undecorated areas to be polished, such as bangle bracelets or large pendants, the pendant drill alone would meet your needs.

3 Materials

Metals

GOLD (melting point 1063°C/1945·4°F.)

Gold has always held a particular fascination for
people all over the world, probably due to its unique
properties. Gold is almost indestructible, it does not
corrode, is highly resistant to acids and is unaffected by
the atmosphere, all of which accounts for its survival
for thousands of years in ancient tombs in many parts
of the world, for example Egypt, China and the biblical
land of Mesopotamia. Its indestructibility is also
responsible for gold having always been highly valued;
as well as being durable, gold always keeps its colour and
shine. It is the most malleable and ductile metal, which
means that it may be beaten to fine gold leaf without
cracking, or pulled to fine wire without breaking. Its
malleability is such that it can be hammered to foil
·00005in thick. The largest gold deposits are in South
Africa and the U.S.S.R., although gold does occur in
almost every country in the world.

Alloys: to produce gold in different colours and
hardnesses and at lower prices, it is mixed or alloyed
with various metals. Pure gold is described as 24 carat

and is too soft for most purposes. The most usual alloys found in Britain are:

22ct: 22 parts gold to 2 parts other metals
18ct: 18 parts gold to 6 parts other metals
 9ct: 9 parts gold to 15 parts other metals.

Of these, 18 carat gold is the most agreeable to work with. Though less economic than 9 carat, it bends, cuts and solders more easily. The exact recipes and proportions of metals alloyed with gold to produce different coloured 18 carat golds varies from one bullion dealer to another. Yellow and red gold are mainly alloyed with silver and copper in different proportions; green gold is usually 30% to 40% silver, or a mixture of silver, cadmium and zinc, and white gold is an alloy of platinum or palladium.

SILVER (melting point 893°C/1640°F.)

The chief disadvantage of gold is, of course, its very high cost. Silver shares many of the properties of gold, but it is considerably cheaper and therefore presents an attractive alternative to gold.

Sterling silver, the form in which silver is sold in Britain, is an alloy of silver and copper, in the proportions of 925 parts silver to 75 parts copper. It is soft and malleable. It bends more easily than 18ct or 9ct gold, though not as easily as 24ct gold. It is ductile, breaking or cracking only slightly more readily than 18ct gold when milled fine. (In order to avoid cracking, silver must be annealed gently and frequently.) It tarnishes, or oxidizes slowly in the air or when heated. The oxidation is a thin black skin on the metal. When it is the result of heating, this skin or 'fire stain' is often difficult to remove. This property also makes silver soldering marginally more hazardous than gold soldering.

Gold and silver solder: solder is an alloy of gold or silver with metals of lower melting point, used to fix together two pieces of silver or gold. Gold solder is available in different colours and different carats. Both silver and gold solders of different melting points are available, usually 'Hard', 'Medium' and 'Easy'.

The hardening and softening of gold and silver: when any non-ferrous metal is worked, it becomes harder and more brittle; this is because the molecules in the metal move closer together. So, when gold or silver are beaten, bent, drawn, stamped or sawn, they become harder and less malleable. In order to soften the metal, it is heated until it becomes a dull red colour, and then cooled. It does not matter whether the cooling process occurs slowly or is effected immediately by quenching in water, the metal remains soft (except in the case of red gold which should be quenched immediately or it will harden slightly). This process is known as *annealing*. Care should be taken not to overheat the metal, because overheating causes melting: the metal shines first and then melts. *Burning:* the metal may shrivel up, burnt before melting. Sometimes an alloyed metal may come to the surface and form fire stain or oxidation which is difficult to remove. This is a hazard chiefly encountered with silver or 9ct gold (Annealing is dealt with in more detail in Chapter 4).

Purchasing gold and silver: in Britain, the sale of gold is restricted by law. For the purpose of making jewellery, gold is sold only to manufacturing jewellers and to colleges which are registered with the Bank of England. So, as a student, you would have to enrol at an Adult Education college, or at an Art School in order to buy gold for making jewellery. The metals are sold in several different forms. Both are sold in a variety of gauges in both sheet and wire. In Britain, sheet is measured according to the Birmingham Metal Gauge Scale, also called 'Shakespeare's Gauge'. It is graded from one to forty which is the equivalent of ·216mm to 7·620mm. Wire is measured according to the Standard Wire Gauge 450 to 1 being the equivalent of 0·25mm to 7·620mm. In the United States the Brown and Sharpe Standard sheet and wire gauge is used (B & S). Like the Standard Wire Gauge, the higher the number, the smaller the gauge. It runs from 40 to 1; the equivalent of ·081mm to 7·341mm. (A table of all three gauges is given on page 147.) Rod and tubing are available in round, triangular and half-round section. Ready-made accessories and 'findings', such as brooch pin catches and hinges, earclip fittings, stone collets, bolt rings, chains, or hollow spheres are also available. When buying gold, specify the carat, colour, gauge and form.

PLATINUM (melting point 1773·5°C/3224·3°F.)

Platinum is a whitish metal much harder than gold or silver. Unlike gold and silver, platinum is a relatively new metal. It was probably first discovered in Colombia, South America in the 16th century, but remained virtually unknown till large deposits were found in the Ural Mountains of Russia in the early 19th century. However, it was not until this century that it began to be extensively used in jewellery, because its extreme hardness makes it difficult to work. It is hardest of the precious metals and therefore difficult to roll thinner or to cut. It does not tarnish and retains a high polish, though it is difficult to polish. It combines very easily with iron; therefore it is important always to pickle it before annealing. The sale of platinum is not restricted by law, it is however usually more expensive than gold.

Purchasing platinum: available in the same gauges of sheet and wire as silver and gold, but few 'findings' because there is not a great demand for platinum from bullion dealers.

COPPER (melting point 1083°C/1981·4°F.)

Copper can be used for jewellery and often is used by beginners because it is cheap; but it is not an easy material to handle. It is more brittle than gold or silver and cannot be drawn or rolled as fine as either. It is harder than gold or silver, making it more difficult to bend. Copper tarnishes in the open air after a few hours. When heated, it oxidizes badly, forming a thick, flaky skin.

Alloys: copper and zinc form brass; copper and tin, bronze.

Purchasing copper: copper is available in many different forms from non-ferrous metal dealers, where it is sold mainly for industrial purposes. It is obtainable in sheet, wire and tube form, the gauge being measured in inches or fractions of an inch.

STEEL (melting point of iron 1539°C/2802°F.)

Steel (a ferrous metal) is an alloy of iron and carbon, containing up to 1·7% carbon. It is harder than any of the other metals, which makes it difficult to work. It is occasionally used for jewellery, but it is suitable only for simple cut out or stamped out work. It does not tarnish. It has a very high melting point.

NICKEL (melting point 1445°C/2651°F.)

Nickel is a base metal, as opposed to a precious metal (such as gold or silver), or an alloy (such as steel or pewter). It is a hard metal, seventh in the scale of ductility, gold being the most ductile metal. It is highly resistant to oxidation and corrosion, it can be cast, forged, machined, welded, brazed and soldered. It becomes work-hardened and must be annealed carefully to soften it. It should be heated slowly to avoid cracking from the sudden release of tension. It can be cooled gradually in the air, or quenched but some alloys of nickel must be quenched immediately, because slow cooling may cause them to crack. Nickel may be soldered with silver solder or lead solder; silver solder is preferable. Being extremely hard, a coarse polishing compound is necessary. Rouge is too soft to have any effect on it, but a high mirror finish can be achieved with white porthos. Nickel is used mainly to alloy with other metals, to increase their hardness without reducing their ductility.

Alloy: the nickel alloy most suitable for jewellery is nickel silver, sometimes known as 'German silver'. It is an alloy of nickel, copper, and zinc. The proportions vary but they are usually in the area of: copper 62% to nickel 33% to zinc 5%. Its melting point is 1071°C/1960°F. It contains no silver, but is a pleasing white colour, resists oxidation at high temperatures, resists corrosion and takes a high polish.

PEWTER

Pewter is an alloy, the chief component of which is tin. Old pewter often had a high lead content, and because of this becomes dull and grey in colour. Today the lead alloy is no longer used and has been replaced by Britannia metal.

BRITANNIA METAL is an alloy of tin (91%), antimony (7%) and copper (2%). Tin gives the metal a sheen, resistance to corrosion, ductility, and prevents excessive oxidation in casting. Antimony hardens and whitens the metal. Also it expands on cooling which causes castings to have sharp, clear impressions from the mold. Copper is added for ductility and hardness. Britannia metal does not work-harden, therefore annealing is not necessary. Because it is soft, the metal will clog a fine file, and so you should use a coarse one, and run it over a piece of chalk first. Solder with soft solder, or tin solder, but check that its melting point is below that of the Britannia metal. Hold the work piece together with soft iron wire for soldering. Do not use a soldering iron, because there is considerable danger of burning a hole in the metal before the solder runs. Use a blow pipe or torch to heat it. Medium grade steel wool removes file marks and scratches; thereafter polish with tripoli and rouge. Pewter and Britannia metal are suitable for engraving and embossing.

The relative hardness of metals and stones is usually measured with a system known as Mohs' Scale, after its originator Friedrich Mohs, a German mineralogist. Mohs' Scale measures the hardness of any material by its ability to be scratched by another. Note that hard metals will take a higher polish than soft ones. (The scale is given overleaf.)

Gemstones

Gemstones and pearls are the materials traditionally associated with jewellery; it is often thought that all gemstones are prohibitively expensive, but this is not so. 'Semi-precious stones' (a misnomer generally applied to all gemstones apart from the top four, rubies, sapphires, emeralds and diamonds), encompass a huge variety of prices. The agate family in particular provides a wide range of different coloured stones which are not at all costly, eg moss agate, cornelian, chrysoprase and onyx. All these are partially opaque stones and are normally cut 'en cabochon', ie not faceted. (Stone faceting was developed to exploit the properties of reflection, and refraction of light.) Among the many faceted gemstones, purple amethysts and green-blue zircons are common and therefore often inexpensive. The opaque stones, turquoise, malachite and lapis lazuli are also available at reasonable prices, though good quality lapis and turquoise can be extremely costly. A list of gemstones, their groupings, characteristics and hardness appears overleaf.

BUYING STONES

The quality and therefore price of a gemstone is determined by various factors, namely colour, reflection, refraction and clarity.

A faceted stone should be free of scratches or chips on the outside surface. The best quality stones are free of bubbles, blemishes, inclusions or interior cracks. Emeralds are an exception, as clear emeralds hardly ever occur. With most stones, a rich, deep tone is more highly valued than a pale or very dark colour. The colour should be uniform throughout the stone.

The standards by which quality is assessed are useful to know, but personal preferences are equally important. For example, rich deep-blue sapphires fetch the highest prices, but many people prefer the softer, paler tones.

Mohs' scale

A rough idea of Mohs' scale of hardness may be obtained from a comparison of the following: finger nail – about $2\frac{1}{2}$; copper coin – about 3; window glass – about $5\frac{1}{2}$; knife blade – about 6; steel file – about $6\frac{1}{2}$.

2–$2\frac{1}{2}$	Amber
2–3	Ivory and Bone
$2\frac{1}{2}$	Tortoiseshell
$2\frac{1}{2}$–3	Bakelite
	Gold
$2\frac{1}{2}$–$3\frac{1}{2}$	Pearl
$3\frac{1}{2}$	Azurite
	Coral
	Jet
	Malachite
4	Fluorspar
5	Obsidian
5–$6\frac{1}{2}$	Opal
$5\frac{1}{2}$–6	Sodalite
6	Feldspar / Moonstone / Labradonte
	Turquoise / Lapis Lazuli / Aventurine
6–$6\frac{1}{2}$	Marcasite
	Pyrites
$6\frac{1}{2}$–7	Chalcedony
	Jadeite
	Peridot
7	Quartz
$6\frac{1}{2}$–$7\frac{1}{2}$	Garnet
$(7\frac{1}{2}$–$8)$	(Beryl)
7	Amethyst
	Citrine
	Topaz (Quartz)
	Rock Crystal (Quartz)
	Smoky Quartz (Quartz)
	Moss Agate
	Chrysoprase
	Cornelian
	Rose Quartz
	Onyx
	Tiger's Eye
8	Spinel
	Emerald
	Topaz (true)
$8\frac{1}{2}$	Chrysoberyl (Cat's Eye)
9	Sapphire ⎱ Corundum
	Ruby ⎰
10	Diamond

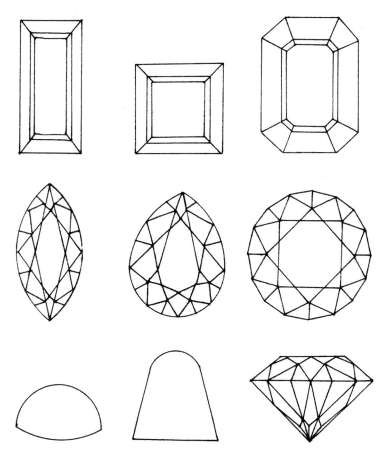

11 The most common gem cuts: left to right,
above: baguette; square; trap, step or emerald
centre: marquise; pendeloque; brilliant
below: medium cabochon; steep cabochon; brilliant cut (side elevation)

The refractive and reflective properties of a stone are vital to its beauty. Stones are faceted in order to allow the maximum amount of light to enter the stone, to be reflected and split into the different component colours of clear light. A stone which sparkles is described as having 'fire'. A badly cut stone will allow the light to pass straight through; from the top, the facets at the base of the stone will appear blank like 'windows'.

Emeralds and *opals* are very fragile and brittle, they will break very easily if subjected to a sudden change of temperature. *Moonstones* are very soft and will scratch easily. *Malachite, turquoise* and *lapis lazuli* are all very soft, and are easily chipped or scratched.

It is advisable always to avoid stones with chips, flaws, cracks etc, because they are more vulnerable and likely to break when being set.

Pearls

These can be divided into three categories: natural, cultured and false. Natural and cultured pearls are formed in various mollusc shells, oysters, mussels and

31

giant clams, for example. Natural pearls grow without assistance from man, cultured pearls are formed round mother-of-pearl beads introduced into the shells by man. Natural pearls are still fished in the Persian Gulf, and off the coasts of Ceylon and North Australia. Fresh water or river pearls are also natural pearls, they are formed in fresh water mussels and are still collected in quantity in Scotland. The majority of cultured pearls come from Japan, where they are produced in such quantities that they are available at reasonable prices.

The value of a pearl depends upon its size and lustre. Natural pearls are more costly than cultured, but owing to the quantity of the latter, and the impossibility of discerning at a glance between a natural and a cultured pearl, even natural ones do not command high prices, unless they are very large. Large, perfectly spherical pearls with a fine lustre command the highest prices. The least expensive are the knobbly and irregular baroque pearls, which includes most river pearls. The lustre is caused by the refraction of light by the edges of the over-lapping plates of nacre or mother-of-pearl which form round the nucleus. A section through a pearl is like an onion. The difference between a drilled natural pearl and a cultured one is difficult to discern by eye, but can easily be tested with an endiscope, an instrument which passes a light through the drilled hole in the centre of the pearl; if the pearl is natural the light will pass through the hole, because the natural layers of nacre or mother-of-pearl reflect it, but it will not pass through a cultured one because the central mother-of-pearl bead does not have concentric layers of nacre and therefore absorbs the light. Undrilled pearls are identified by X-ray.

Pearls can have pink, blue, green or yellow tinges, they can also be black (though many black pearls are dyed). They are available from about 3mm diameter and are sold undrilled, half drilled, fully drilled or in halves.

False pearls have no mother-of-pearl coating. Artificial pearls used to be made by coating glass beads with a solution of fish scales and lacquer, but they are now usually made of plastic with a plastic coating. It is easy to distinguish an artificial pearl from a natural or cultured one by testing it on your teeth. The layers of mother-of-pearl feel gritty, whilst an artificial one is smooth.

Other materials: ivory; horn; tortoiseshell; wood; acryllic resin and perspex; enamel; mother-of-pearl and shells.

Many materials can be used for making jewellery. This

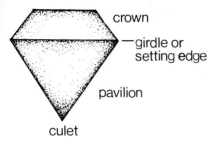

crown

girdle or setting edge

pavilion

culet

12 Section of a cut stone

section gives some suggestions for materials which seem particularly suitable, but there are many others which may appeal to you.

Ivory is usually elephant tusk, but can also be walrus tusk or even mammoth tusk, which was excavated in Siberia in the nineteenth century. Horn comes from a wide range of animals. New pieces of horn and ivory are not easy to find, but junk shops sometimes have horns or tusks which have been hunting trophies and old knife handles which also provide a possible source. Both horn and ivory are easy to work and can be treated in the same way. They are soft and can be cut with the piercing saw, filed and polished with fine files and calico, cotton or wool mops. The particular appeal of horn is its translucency which is shown well if you cut a thin sheet along the direction of the grain. Ivory and horn react to sudden changes of temperature by either warping or cracking, so these should be avoided, as should extreme heat or cold.

Tortoiseshell is also difficult to obtain new, but can be found in junk shops. It is softer than horn, and should not be exposed to extremes of temperature.

Hard woods, such as walnut, boxwood or ebony are attractive used in jewellery either for their colour or their grain pattern, or both. Most hard woods can be obtained from good wood merchants, though ebony is very difficult to find new. The wood can be cut with a piercing saw, filed and polished with wet and dry emery paper, finishing with a very fine grade. It is inadvisable to polish wood with a polishing mop on the polishing machine, because the force of the machine will tend to gouge out the softer parts of the grain.

Shells can be used in many different ways, either whole or cut up and inlaid or framed with metal. Mother-of-pearl is a soft and rather brittle substance, which has been built up in layers. It can be cut with a piercing saw and filed with fine files, but care must be taken, as it chips easily.

Acryllic is a relatively new material, now widely used in jewellery. It is produced in many different colours, both transparent and opaque, in many different gauges of sheet. Some colours are also available in rods. Acryllic resin, together with colour pigments and hardener, can be bought from a few acrylic dealers. They are also sold in kits at craftshops and toy shops. An inlay effect can be achieved with the liquid resin. First you have to make a flat-backed metal frame, to which you solder a cut-out metal pattern which lies more than two millimetres proud of the backplate. The liquid resin must then be poured into the frame, and when it has hardened, ground down flush with the metal, polished with fine emery paper and sugar paper and finally with rouge. Acryllic sheet can be cut easily with a piercing saw, but it has a low melting point, so the friction of the blade will cause it to melt rather like wax. To avoid this, cut very slowly or play a jet of cold water onto the cutting line. To finish off a cut edge, first use an old, fine-toothed file, then fine emery paper and polish with rouge on a soft cotton or wool mop. If it is heated to 175°–190°C, acryllic becomes malleable and can be bent into any shape, in which it hardens as it cools.

4 Basic techniques

This chapter outlines all the basic techniques which will be treated in more detail in later chapters.

Piercing and sawing

Sawing metal with a piercing saw seems difficult and uncontrolled initially, but with a little practice it soon becomes easier. When the skill of sawing has been mastered it is the most accurate method of cutting metal. Alternatives to sawing sheet metal, such as using a guillotine or shears, not only lack the flexibility of the saw, but also cause distortion on both sides of the cut edge.

A jeweller's adjustable piercing saw frame is used with steel sawblades. The blade thickness is selected according to the thickness of the metal to be cut. For general use 2/0 blades are the most useful; for very fine decorative cut-out work 4/0 or 5/0 is advisable, whilst a 1 or 2 is useful for heavier work. If the blade is too thick for the metal, it will tend to jam and break frequently.

To fix the blade in the saw frame, with the handle nearest you, loosen the clamp screws at each end of the frame, insert the blade at the far end and tighten the screw. The teeth of the blade must be pointing downwards towards the handle. Place the end of the frame against the bench and apply pressure to the saw handle so that the frame is bent slightly inwards; then tighten the second clamp. When the sawframe is released from pressure it should hold the blade absolutely taut.

Hold the piece to be cut, on or against the bench-pin with one hand, and guide the saw with the other. Hold the saw firmly, but not in a clenched grasp; sometimes resting your thumb on the lower clamp helps guide the frame (**13**). In order to saw a clean, regular line it is important to relax and to saw rhythmically. Remember that only the downward stroke onto the metal cuts as the teeth all face downwards. Forcing the saw frame forward will cause the blade to jam or break, so just guide it. It is equally important to hold the metal firmly. A slip could also cause the blade to snap. A flat piece of metal can be held flat against the pin with your hand, but hold very small pieces in the parallel pliers or hand vice. Cut a small V-shaped notch in the pin against which you can rest the metal. This is extremely useful for support. To start sawing, make a few upward strokes first. This makes a groove which is then cut by the downward stroke. When sawing round a curve, never force the blade: for a tight curve saw up and down at the same spot gently, moving the metal round. This allows the blade to cut itself enough space to turn on its own axis. Try to keep the sawframe upright and at the same angle all the time: if you let it lean to one side, the edge will naturally be sloped and also the blade is likely to break. Initially, it is unlikely that your sawblades will survive long enough to blunt, but renew the blade if it ceases to cut easily.

MARKING OUT THE METAL

Tools: sharp pointed scriber, compasses, metal ruler, carbon paper.

Sawing accurate lines by eye takes considerable practice, so it is always advisable to mark out the metal before cutting it. Initially, when sawing a straight line, it helps to scribe two straight lines with a narrow gap between them, along which you saw. Always draw straight lines with a metal ruler, not a wooden one. When cutting to a marked design, cut round the line, not along it, otherwise you will have no guide to file up to. For complex designs, draw up the design accurately and to scale, then trace it on to the metal surface. There are a number of ways of tracing a design onto metal, perhaps the simplest being with carbon paper. Having transferred the design with carbon paper, go over the

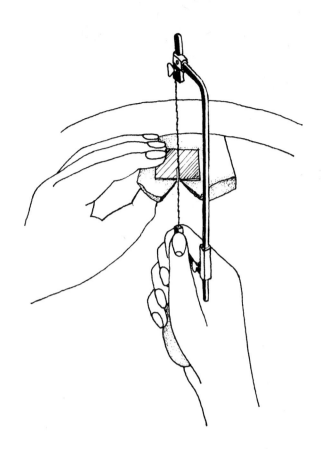

13 Sawing with a piercing saw

blue carbon lines with a sharp metal scriber to incise the pattern more clearly and permanently on the metal. To pierce out an enclosed area, drill a hole, free one end of the sawblade from the frame, insert this through the drilled hole and refix it to the sawframe. To facilitate sawing, lubricate the blade with spit, candle grease or oil.

Drilling

Drilling is done with a hand drill, an Archimedes drill or an electric pendant drill. The hand drill and electric drill are used with twist drills, while a spade drill is used in the Archimedes drill. Neither the hand drill nor the electric drill presents any difficulties. Always mark the point where the drill hole is to be with a small recess made with the scriber point, or any other sharp instrument. The tip of the drill will lodge in the recess instead of slipping over the metal and scratching it. It also ensures that the hole is made in the right place. The drills should be sharp. If progress is slow and the drill is not sending up a small spiral of metal it should be replaced or sharpened carefully on the India stone.

37

Initially it seems difficult to handle the Archimedes drill, but it does not take long to master. First fasten a spade drill in the chuck. Hold the tool with the string fully extended, then revolve the crossbar, so that the string wraps round the top of the drill stick and the crossbar rises. Hold the drill by the crossbar, with the central stick between the first and second fingers of your right hand. Place the drill tip on the point to be drilled, hold the drill vertical and push the crossbar down with gentle pressure from the fingers of your right hand, which is resting on it. The pressure should be light because when the crossbar reaches its lowest point, the string begins to coil round the stick again. As the crossbar rises, no pressure should be exerted on it. It sounds complicated, but the necessary light rhythmic movement with your right hand is soon acquired.

Filing

Filing is also a cutting technique, a way of removing metal, but it is mainly a 'cleaning up' process, used for trueing up a shape which has been sawn or shaped with the pliers, or for removing scratches and excess solder.

A wide variety of files is available; different sizes, shapes and cuts. The most useful ones are listed in Chapter 2. All the teeth of the file lie in the same direction, facing away from the handle, and so it is only the forward stroke which cuts.

When selecting a file it is important to choose one suited to the job in terms of size, shape and cut, eg for a long edge of thick metal, use a large flat-sided file; the cut depends upon the amount of metal to be removed. The half round ring file is the most useful. For fine work use a needle file, choosing the shape to suit the work.

Filing is not difficult, but it is deceptive. For example, when straightening a concave edge, you are liable to find that you have removed the ends, thus making a convex edge instead. Hold the file firmly and keep it level; as with sawing, do not force the file, just guide it, trying to avoid dipping to one side or the other (**14**). Do not make the common mistake of using too small a file. Use long strokes, not short scratchy ones. If a lot of metal is to be removed, it should be done with a very coarse file to start with, changing to finer ones for finishing off.

To file a straight line, place the file slightly diagonally across the metal edge. It is difficult to file a flat edge with the file lying along the metal, because the pressure will tend to vary. When filing up a curved surface, do not use small straight strokes, but follow the shape of

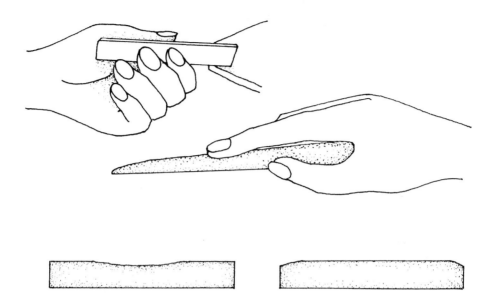

14 Filing:
above left: holding the metal to be filed
centre right: holding the file
below: concave and convex results of filing – to be avoided

the metal, filing round the curve with the file across, or at 90° to the metal.

Repoussé

The following sections deal with the methods of shaping metal by applying pressure to produce a new shape. Repoussé work is raising a shape or design in relief on one side of the metal by beating the reverse side with a hammer and punches, whilst the metal is supported by a slightly yielding material such as pitch or lead. This is one of the oldest decorative techniques used in metalwork.

The tools needed are a selection of doming punches (round headed punches and some other shapes are available from jewellers' suppliers, although any shape you need can easily be filed up at the end of a steel rod); a hammer, preferably a chasing hammer, and a lead or pitch block. The thickness of the metal that you use depends upon the depths and complexity of your design. The thinnest practicable gauge is G.8 BMG or ·546mm and thickest is G.18 BMG or 1·5mm. Anything thinner will tend to crack, whilst anything thicker will not yield.

It is important to secure the metal to the support you are using. If it is a pitch block, warm the pitch so that the top surface melts, but does not burn and press the annealed metal down on to it, so that it is held at the edges and there are no hollows under the metal. If you are using a lead block, beat a flat area on the lead block and then hammer the metal sheet onto it with a mallet until it is held well by the lead.

Fix the design to the metal with a piece of wax at each corner, and trace the design onto the metal with a fine pointed punch or tracer. Having traced out the design, fill it out with the punches which will produce the height of relief that you want. A flat punch will produce low relief whilst a rounded one produces deeper modelling. To achieve a smooth continuous line takes time and practice, but it is achieved when you can keep a steady rhythm, moving the punch evenly all the time whilst beating it steadily. There is no need to hit the punch very hard; the important thing is for the stroke to be steady. Repoussé techniques are treated in more detail in Chapter 6.

Bending and shaping with the pliers

There are two ways of bending flat metal into shapes, for example into rings or bangles. The first is by using pliers which are made in several different sizes and in a variety of jaw shapes; the second is by beating the metal on an anvil or a mould. Hammering a piece into shape is a technique associated with silversmithing rather than jewellery making. It has to be used when the design of a ring or bangle includes thick gauge metal which is too thick to be bent with pliers. The pliers are the most useful tools for shaping pieces because of the high degree of accuracy you can achieve with them, without marking the metal. This is particularly important when you are making stone settings known as collets. As with any skill, it seems difficult initially, but with practice and a systematic approach, the results will soon prove rewarding. It is particularly satisfying when you can turn up a ring or collet accurately.

The half round pliers are the most useful. If you cannot buy a pair small enough for making small collets, ie 3–4mm diameter collets, file down the jaws of a larger pair to the required size. Always use half round pliers to turn up a curve; flat pliers mark the inside of the curve and round nosed ones mark the outside.

Round nosed pliers are used for turning up a small quantity of tiny links or jump rings; flat pliers are used for turning up angles and straight sided collets for square or rectangular stones.

Circles are particularly difficult to perfect with pliers. To true up rings and straight sided round collets of 7mm diameter or more, tap them on the conical steel tube with a hide or wooden mallet. For trueing up round collets with tapered sides, a collet plate and collet punch is available and is extremely useful. Bending and shaping techniques are described in more detail in Chapters 6, 7 and 8.

The heating processes of soldering and annealing

SOLDERING

Jewellery is generally constructed of many small pieces soldered together. Carving or piercing a piece from a solid lump of metal is costly, wasteful of materials, time consuming and it is impossible to arrive at the delicacy or detail achieved with constructional techniques. Separate sections are sometimes riveted or hinged together but soldering is the most useful method of joining two or more pieces.

There are two types of soldering; hard and soft. In both, the solder is made of a metal alloy which has a lower melting point than the non-ferrous metal to be joined. Soft soldering, sometimes known as lead or tin solder, is widely used in electrical engineering, but is unsuitable for jewellery on two counts. Firstly, the chief component of the solder is lead, which under some circumstances attacks gold or silver, and secondly, a relatively large quantity of solder has to be used to form a strong bond. For hard soldering, silver and gold solders are used. A strong bond is formed by a fine membrane of solder between the two surfaces. It is suitable for jewellery because the join is extremely strong and should be invisible. Careful preparation is essential to achieve this strong and invisible join.

Tools: solder snips/shears; borax; borax dish, brush and water; emery paper; binding wire; cotter pins; charcoal block; asbestos block; blowpipe.

To prepare two surfaces for soldering
1 Both surfaces must be completely clean; oxidation or grease, even from the fingers, can prevent the solder from running. Cleaning should be done either by pickling in acid and rinsing well in water, or by exposing new metal with a fine file or emery.

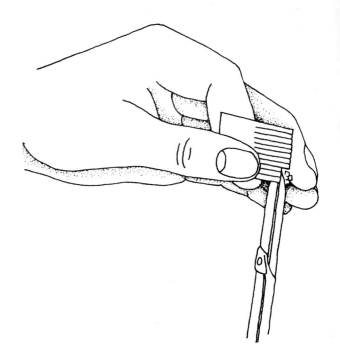

2 Both surfaces must fit each other exactly. The joint
on a ring shank should fit together so tightly that it is
hardly visible even before soldering. If necessary hold
the joint in place with binding wire, cotter pins, or
sprung soldering tweezers.
3 Fluxing: to keep the joint clean and prevent
oxidation when it is heated, paint the joint with borax
paste. For the paste, grind the borax cone with water
on a rough earthenware dish until it is the consistency
of thin cream. Also dip the solder paillons in borax.
4 To cut the solder paillons: the easiest way of doing
this is illustrated. Rest the solder against the first finger
of your left hand (if you are right-handed) when cutting
across. This will prevent the tiny squares of metal
jumping everywhere. Always prepare slightly more
solder than you think you need, because it is irritating
to have to cut more in the middle of a soldering
operation (**15**).
5 Placing the solder: having brought together the
surfaces to be soldered so that they form a perfect join
with no gaps or overlaps, place the boraxed solder
across the join so that it touches both sides. Avoid
filling gaps with solder as it often flows out during a later
heating.

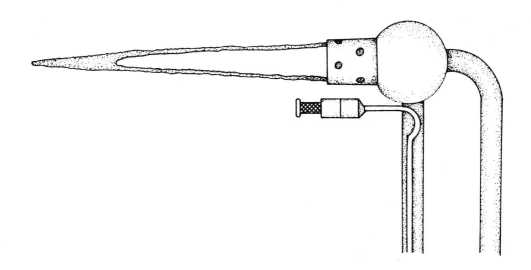

16 Soldering flame

6 Heating: the flame generally used for soldering is a mixture of gas and air, and should be adjusted to a soft blue flame; a yellow flame indicates insufficient air. Inside the blue flame is a darker blue cone. The point at the end of that inner cone is the hottest part of the flame; inside the inner cone the flame is colder (**16**). Heat the piece very gently to set the borax, playing a soft flame over the whole piece. Sudden or intense heat will cause the solder to jump off. Concentrate the flame on the whole area round the join, avoiding direct heat on the solder, as, being smaller, it will tend to melt into a ball before the surrounding metal is hot enough to allow it to run. The solder should run in a sudden shining flow, filling the join, when the metal has reached a dull red colour. Remove the heat.

7 First remove iron binding wire then pickle in acid or alum.

ANNEALING

The atomic structure of non-ferrous metals is such that when the metal is worked, for example hammered or bent, the molecules are compressed closer together. In other words, when the metal is worked, it becomes harder, more brittle and less malleable and therefore

43

more difficult to handle. This is easily remedied by heating it to a high temperature, a process known as annealing. Nine carat gold should be quenched immediately in cold water, but with other carat golds, and silver, the speed of cooling is unimportant, as once they are heated to the right temperature, they are softened. It is usually necessary to anneal a piece several times during its manufacture. It does not take long to get the feel of the metal and to realize when it has hardened and should be annealed to facilitate handling.

To anneal, heat the metal, either held in the air or on a charcoal block, until it is a dull red colour. Repeated overheating can cause it to burn up. Melting is another hazard; if the surface of the metal becomes shiny, remove the heat immediately.

If the piece to be annealed is already half constructed, there are two important considerations. The first is that the solder holding the piece together will melt at a lower temperature than the metal itself, and so it is vital not to overheat it. The second is equally important: when metal is worked and has hardened, there are tensions in the metal which can be removed by annealing, but it is essential to heat the piece evenly to avoid releasing the tensions in one area faster than in another, causing it to distort. For example, a ring which has been bent up from a flat strip, will open up if one side is heated faster than the other. This is a factor which must also be taken into account when soldering.

Pickling

When the piece has been soldered or annealed, the vitrified borax and the oxide on unfluxed areas are removed in an acid pickle. As explained in Chapter 2, the pickle is either sulphuric acid 10% dilution or alum 30% dilution, heated in a pyrex dish or bowl. The article should be left in the pickle until the oxidation has disappeared. With alum this takes slightly longer than sulphuric acid: about two or three minutes. The pickle should be renewed from time to time as it ceases to function eventually. Never put iron or steel into the pickle as they will cause discolouration of the work. This means removing iron binding wire and *always* using brass or copper tweezers. Always wash the piece thoroughly in water. It is worth keeping separate dishes of pickle for different metals, because silver, for example, tends to become plated with gold when pickled in the same solution.

Finishing and polishing

The importance of finishing and polishing to the final look of a piece is often underestimated or neglected. It is simple to get a good shine on the most accessible areas of metal, but much more skilful to achieve a really good overall finish. Of course sometimes a textured or matt finish is preferable to a high polish; it is a matter of taste. Either way, the finishing can make or mar a piece.

Polishing is the process of removing marks and scratches with an abrasive, whose fine scratches are in turn removed by a yet finer abrasive (ie a file or polishing compound). Try to avoid marking the piece whilst making it; deep plier marks or deep file scratches are difficult to remove effectively. In order to remove them, a layer of metal equal in thickness to the depth of the scratch must be removed which can easily alter the intended shape and design of the piece. To achieve a good finish, a systematic and thorough approach is essential. This means that each component piece should be finished as far as possible before it is soldered to another part. It is often very difficult to get at areas in a completed piece which could have been cleaned easily before assembly. For example, a flat piece of metal to be soldered to a larger metal plate can be buffed flat more easily before assembly; this avoids scratching the back plate when filing up the edges *in situ*.

Tools: files suitable to the size and form of the piece; emery paper Grades 2 and 0; crocus paper; polishing motor – pendant drill; bristle brushes; cotton mops; lamb's wool mops; water of Ayr stone; felts for flat surfaces.

Polishing compounds: tripoli; pink porthos; rouge; polishing string.

Clean the metal of excess solder, using needle files, water of Ayr stone or a riffler file to reach inaccessible or concave areas. Remove deep scratches with a suitable file or emery paper. If the marks are deep it is clearly a waste of time to start with a fine file or emery; graduate to finer grades, having removed the worst. When filing or using emery, don't concentrate only on the immediate area of the scratch or dent, but cover a wider area in order to fade out the file marks; otherwise you risk making a worse blemish. Always wrap the emery tightly round a file or emery stick, as described in Chapter 2, and secure it with binding wire. This enables you to apply an even pressure to the piece, whereas using a wad of folded emery tends to result in uneven depressions and bumps on the surface. As with filing, in order to achieve a sharp, clean finish, it is important to use the emery firmly and boldly, taking care not to round off corners. Short tentative little strokes will be very time-consuming and result in a rather messy look. When the surface has been finished with Grade 0 emery or Ayr stone, and there are no visible big scratches, the piece is ready for polishing. Avoid trying to remove marks with the polishing machine. If when polishing you find some scratches you have overlooked, file or emery them out and then continue polishing. The polishing motor is extremely powerful and can remove large areas of metal which will completely distort the look of the piece.

POLISHING

When the piece is ready for polishing, the first thing to do is to choose the right polishing brush or felt. For flat surfaces a felt wheel 1in thick is suitable, whilst a 2½in diameter bristle brush, or 3in diameter coarse calico mop are suitable for most other work.

Stand in front of the motor, with the mop revolving towards you from the top (**17**). The mop or brush is charged with a block of tripoli or porthos held against it for a few moments. Tripoli and porthos are solid blocks of abrasive and grease compounds. Tripoli is advised for gold and silver, but pink porthos which is sold for polishing harder metals such as steel is much cleaner and very effective so long as it is used sparingly. The object to be polished is offered up to the mop, near the bottom of the mop. It should be kept moving to avoid over-concentration on one spot, which results in unwanted bumps and depressions. Also avoid rounding off corners.

There is one risk to guard against. The wheel revolves at considerable speed, consequently there is the danger that the piece of jewellery will get caught in it and either bend or spin out of your hands, an unnerving experience and bad for the piece you are working on. Never polish chain on the polishing motor without first wrapping it round a piece of thick card or soft wood and securing the loose ends. The two main reasons for other sorts of jewellery getting caught are either that too much pressure has been applied, or that part of the piece, especially a sharp protrusion, is being held against the direction of rotation. Avoid sticking sharp points in the mop; they may bend or catch and spin the piece out of your hands. Remember too that long hair or loose ribbons can easily get caught in the motor, with uncomfortable results.

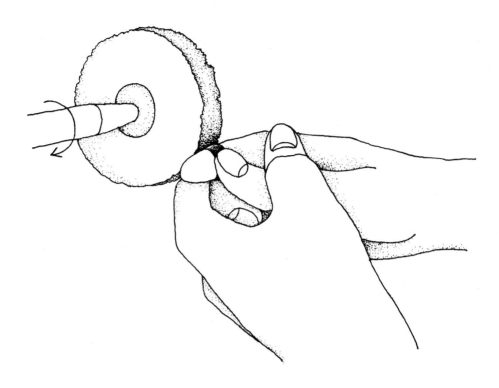

17 Position for polishing a ring

When an overall polish is achieved with the tripoli or porthos, wash all the polishing grease off with hot water and soap or detergent; an old toothbrush is often useful at this stage. Dry the piece and then repeat the polishing process with a fine cotton or lambswool mop. For very fine work it is preferable to use the flexible shaft drill or pendant drill fitted with little hand brushes and mops; the best way of polishing drilled or pierced holes is by drawing linen thread charged with tripoli or rouge through the holes.

In time, the polishing wheels become clogged with polishing compound, and deposit black greasy lumps on the metal. This can be easily remedied by holding a coarse file against the revolving wheel for a few seconds. Be careful to keep tripoli and rouge mops separate; obviously a rouge mop will cease to give such a fine polish if it is contaminated with tripoli or porthos.

5 Piercing & soldering

The basic methods for piercing and soldering have already been described in Chapter 4. In this chapter, three pieces, two pendants and a ring, which are pierced and soldered are described. I have also included a list of things which can go wrong when soldering, and how to avoid them.

The first piece is a simple pendant with a design cut out from the centre, and a loop soldered to the top (**18**). To make the pendant you need a piece of G16 silver sheet 2 × 1in. The tools and equipment needed are as follows: a sharp pencil and paper for drawing the design (graph paper is useful for drawing regular ovals or for drawing the two sides of a symmetrical shape). A draughtsman's stencil of curves is also useful for these purposes. Carbon paper, a scriber, an Archimedes drill stock or pendant drill stock and a drill at least 1mm in diameter. Saw frame and gauge 2/0 blades, half round file and half round needle file, both Cut 2. A burnisher, an emery stick and emery paper Grades 2/0 and 00, and soldering equipment. The soldering equipment needed is: a charcoal block, borax cone, dish and brush, cotter pins, shears and heat source.

First draw out the design on squared paper, and fix it with wax or self-adhesive tape over a piece of carbon

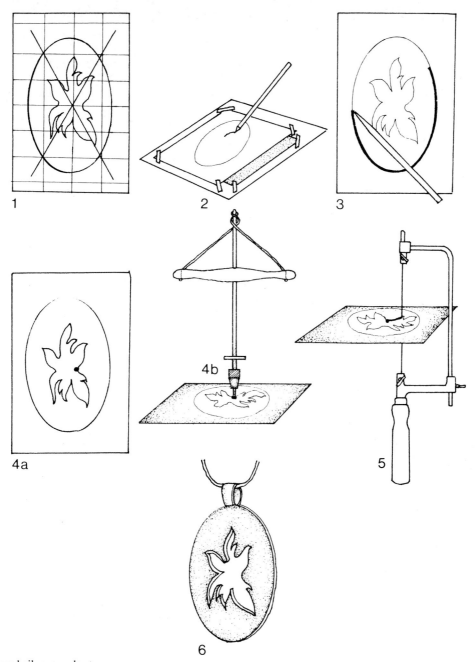

18 Pierced silver pendant
1 Drawing out the pendant on graph paper
2 Tracing the design onto the metal with carbon paper
3 Scribing the traced line into the metal
4a Marking a hole to be drilled inside the outline
4b Drilling with the Archimedes drill
5 Piercing out the central design
6 The finished piece

paper and onto the metal (**18, 1**). Then trace the design firmly onto the metal, using a fine scriber (**18, 2**). Remove the paper and go over the traced carbon line with the scriber so that it is clearly scratched into the metal (**18, 3**). If you use a design which incorporates a circle, draw a circle directly onto the metal with the dividers. Mark a point with the scriber, just inside the outline of the central pattern and drill it (**18, 4**). Mark the point deep enough for the tip of the drill to rest in so that it does not slip over the metal to start with. Fix the sawblade in the upper saw clamp, thread the blade through the drilled hole, and fix the blade in the lower clamp (**18, 5**). Rest the silver on the bench pin and saw round the inside of the scribed line. Do not try to cut round sharp angles and corners in one continuous line; instead cut across each one below the point and then cut towards the point from both sides. Having cut out the central piece, saw round the outside of the pendant outline. File the cut edges up to the scribed line, using a half-round needle file Cut 2, for the central part and a large flat file Cut 2 for the outside edge. To smooth the inside edge, burnish it with the burnisher. To do this, hold the burnisher at right angles to the metal, short edge to the metal, and draw it firmly towards you, pressing all the time; this irons out the scratches and leaves a shine (**19**). There is another way of finishing off the inside edges, using the pendant drill or flexible shaft. You need a steel rod approximately 2in long, diameter $\frac{3}{32}$in; an old drill, or the shaft of a small polishing brush would do. Fix it in the hand vice or the engineer's vice with approximately an inch projecting vertically from the top of the vice, and with a Cut 2 sawblade, cut a shaft approximately $\frac{1}{2}$in down the middle of the rod (**20**). Secure the uncut end in the drill chuck. Cut a strip of emery paper slightly less than $\frac{1}{2}$in wide and the length of the sheet of paper, insert one end of the strip in the shaft, start the motor and the paper will wrap itself tightly round the shaft. Now smooth the edge of the silver, holding the emery paper at right angles to the metal, and moving it all the time to avoid making grooves. Cutting a shaft in the rod is not easy until you have mastered sawing, because you will tend to cut a crooked or jagged line. To finish the outside edge for polishing it is better to use an emery stick; the result will be sharper than using the emery roll. The next stage is to polish the pendant. This is best done before the loop is soldered on, because the loop will prevent it from lying flat. First check that the pendant is flat by placing it on the metal flattening stake. If it is not, tap it with the mallet until there are no gaps between the stake and the silver sheet. To remove the

19 Burnishing the edges of a ring

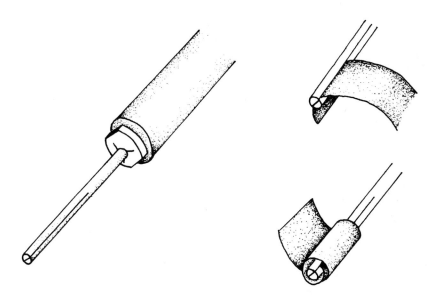

20 Making a split shaft

21 Holding the loop in place with a cotter pin for soldering

scratches, stretch a piece of emery paper over the flattening stake, Grade 2 emery or another grade suitable for the state of the surface. Rub the pendant on it with a circular motion; avoid concentrating on one area of the silver and keep it completely flat. When the biggest scratches have disappeared, repeat the process with a finer emery paper. Continue to do this with progressively finer papers until you have achieved a good shine with crocus paper. The next thing to do is ruin that shine by soldering on the loop.

To make the loop, cut a strip of silver $\frac{3}{32}$ by $\frac{3}{4}$in, either from the remains of the G16 piece or from a piece of finer gauge sheet. File the edges straight, anneal it, and then with the half-round pliers, bend it in half so that the ends touch each other. File it into a wedge shape so that it is wider at the top than at the ends, and file across the ends so that the loop would stand on its own. Next, file a slight curve with the half-round file so that the loop fits the curve of the pendant. To solder the loop to the pendant, place both on the charcoal with the loop in place. Use a cotter pin to keep it in place when soldering (**21**). Borax the join, place two or three small paillons of boraxed solder across the join and heat the pendant gently. Concentrate more heat on the

51

pendant than on the loop because it is larger and will take longer than the loop to reach the temperature at which the solder will run on it. There will also be heat loss through the charcoal, which conducts heat away from the metal where ever they touch. In this case they touch over 50% of the surface area. When the solder has run, pickle and rinse the pendant; remove any excess solder with a file and then water of Ayr stone. To restore the polish you obtained with the crocus paper before soldering, give the piece a final buffing on the polishing wheel.

The second pendant requires more soldering than the first. It is made in three sections which are cut out separately and soldered together (**22**). To make it you will need a sheet of BMG 10 silver and the same tools as the first pendant required.

Draw the three sections out on paper and trace them on to the silver sheet, arranging them so as to make the most economical use of the metal (**22, 1**). Cut round the lines you have scribed, without cutting into them. As in the previous piece, to get the angles between the curves sharp, cut out the whole piece first, by-passing the angles and then cut into the corners from both sides (**22, 2**). Clean up the edges with the files, emery sticks and emery spindle if you have made one. The three pieces should be flat and their top surfaces should be free from scratches. This will be the last good opportunity to polish up the surfaces, as it will be difficult to clean round the curves once the three sections are soldered together. First check that they are flat on the flattening stake, tapping them with the mallet if they are not, in the way described for the first pendant. Then rub the upper surface of each piece and the back of the backplate on emery paper stretched over the flattening stake, (**22, 3**). When you have achieved a scratchless polish on all three, they are ready to be soldered together. To solder all three together at the same time would be hazardous because one part would probably move out of position during heating. Instead, solder the top two pieces together first, rather than the bottom two, because it is easier to heat two units of roughly the same area evenly than to solder a small unit to a large one. Place the middle section on the charcoal, borax it and place the top section in the position in which it is to be soldered. You may find it useful to scribe three or four tiny marks to show the position the pieces should be in. Cut some paillons of medium silver solder about $\frac{1}{16}$ in square; borax them, and with the fluxing brush place four or five of them over the join round the edge of the pendant (**22, 4**). The borax should be the consistency of thin cream and

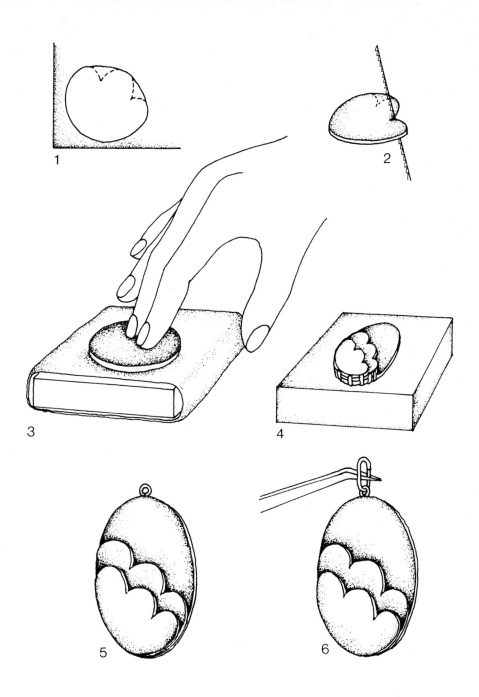

22 Soldered
1 Cut each section out
2 Cut into the angles
3 Rub each part flat
4 Place the solder paillons on the
outside join
5 The assembled piece and jump ring
6 Attach second loop

should keep the paillons in place. If they fall off very easily, play a soft flame over the piece gently, to set the borax. Use a gentle flame to start with, playing it over the whole piece, moving it all the time without letting it linger on the solder. Both pieces should be heated evenly so that the solder will melt and run between the two plates. The top piece will heat faster, because it is smaller and on top. The lower piece is not only a larger area but also the charcoal conducts heat away from its lower surface. When the two pieces are a dull red colour, the solder should melt and flow. If this does not happen, and you see the silver becoming a more brilliant red or beginning to shine, stop and turn to the section on soldering difficulties at the end of this chapter (p. 56). It is very tempting to feel that the solder must run if you heat it just a little more or a little longer, but it is generally disastrous to yield to the temptation.

Pickle and rinse the soldered pieces. Then repeat the process, soldering them to the backplate, using soft solder this time (**22, 4**). Make sure that all the solder joints are strong and sound. The solder should have run all the way through so that no gaps are visible.

To make the jump ring or loop from which the pendant will be suspended you will need a ready-made jump ring or a small length of wire, BWG16. To make the link, bend up a small ring about $\frac{1}{8}$ to $\frac{3}{16}$ in in diameter with the round nosed pliers. Hold the link in the parallel pliers and cut it off the length of wire with the saw; the saw will give a cleaner end for joining than the snips. Hold the link in the parallel pliers and the flat pliers, and ease the ends together to form a close join. Then file a small facet across the join with a needle file, so that a larger part of the link will touch the pendant. Lay the pendant on the charcoal block, face up, and place the jump ring in position so that the facet with the join in the middle touches the pendant. Borax and solder it with soft silver solder, bearing in mind that the jump ring is the smallest part and will heat fastest (**22, 5**). In order to suspend the pendant from a chain so that it lies flat, a second link threaded through the first must be added. With the round nosed pliers, bend a piece of G16 wire into an oblong link, with the join in one of the long sides. Thread this through the existing jump ring and close up the join. Hold the oblong link in the soldering tweezers, borax it and solder it with soft solder (**22, 6**). Concentrate the flame on the oblong link, and keep it away from the soldered join of the jump ring. Pickle and rinse the pendant. If there is any excess solder, file it and grind it off with water of Ayr stone. If the pendant has had to be cleaned of much excess solder, polish it with tripoli or pink porthos on the bristle lathe brush or the felt lathe wheel. If the metal shows signs of bending, support it on a strong piece of card when you offer it to the polishing wheel. Wash off the harsh polishing agent in hot water and detergent. Then finish it with jeweller's rouge on the soft cotton mop.

To make the ring, you will need a strip of silver, $1 \times 2\frac{1}{2}$in BMG14, and $3\frac{1}{2}$in of wire G18 (**23**). The tools needed are the saw, dividers, scriber, triblet, half-round pliers, files and emery paper, the soldering equipment and binding wire.

First make a plain ring $\frac{5}{16}$in wide, following the directions which you will find at the beginning of the next chapter. When it is trued and finished with a fine emery paper, it is ready for the leaf and wire decoration to be added (**23, 1**). On the rest of the sheet of silver, mark out the leaves. With the dividers, measure out the length that the leaves are to be, approximately $\frac{5}{16}$in, then draw in the leaves free-hand with the scriber (**23, 2**). Cut them out with the saw and true them up with a flat needle file. They have to be slightly curved to fit the curve of the ring. To curve them, either bend them with the half round pliers or place them one at a time in one of the middle sized cavities of the doming block, and punch them with a doming punch of at least $\frac{1}{2}$in diameter with the hammer. (The second method is the easier.) (**23, 3**) Clean up each leaf, using an emery stick. When this is done they are ready to solder to the ring. With the half round pliers bend the wire so that the ends are straight, but about $\frac{1}{4}$in at the centre is curved to fit the ring (**23, 4**). It then has to be bent to make the switch-back curve of the pattern (**23, 5**). Having done this, bind the wire to the ring with binding wire and solder that section on with medium solder (**23, 6**). Hold the ring in the soldering tweezers whilst heating it; this is a much quicker method than resting it on the charcoal. When it is soldered, pickle and rinse the piece, having first removed the binding wire. Now that the wire is attached to the ring you can bend it round the ring with the half round pliers and your fingers, to make the pattern shown in the drawing. Solder it in easy stages, leaving at least $\frac{1}{2}$in to play with at both ends. Cut the ends so that they join in a close joint, and solder the join and the wire to the ring at the same time. Clean off any excess solder with the water of Ayr stone. Now place the leaves in position, secure them with binding wire and solder them to the ring with easy solder (**23, 7**). It will probably be easiest to do this in two or three stages. Clean off the excess solder with water of Ayr stone. It is not possible to get a really good polish on the whole ring unless the soldering has been

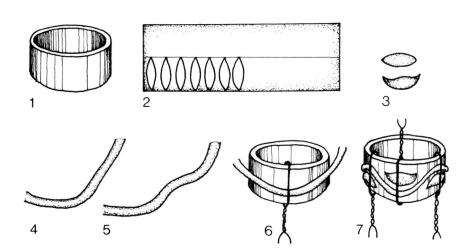

23 Silver ring with applied leaves
1 The ring ready for decoration
2 Cut the leaves from sheet
3 Dome the leaves to the curve of the ring
4 Bend the wire to the curve of the ring
5 & 6 The wire and leaves wired in place for soldering

impeccable and no solder has had to be ground off. It is therefore advisable to finish the ring with a matt texture, either with the Ayr stone or a glass brush (see p. 119). The leaves and wire can be polished, giving a contrast with the matt background. Polish the inside of the ring with tripoli and then with rouge on two separate lathe fingers.

Soldering difficulties

Soldering often presents difficulties initially, which can seem quite inexplicable. For example, the solder won't melt whilst the rest of the piece is about to collapse, or else it runs in the wrong place. Here is a list of possible causes.

A dirty join or greasy solder: even if a piece has been carefully pickled and rinsed, acid or alum can get trapped in the join. The only certain way of making a completely clean join is to expose a fresh layer of metal with a file or emery or by sawing through the join.

Insufficient or weak borax: make sure the borax is the consistency of single cream, and that it covers all the area to be soldered. Don't allow the borax to be contaminated, particularly by rouge or tripoli polishing compounds because they prevent the solder from running. If you have made several attempts at soldering one area and the borax has vitrified into a thick glassy skin, pickle it off and start again.

Oversized solder paillons: generally speaking any paillons of solder over 2mm square are too large and it is better to use smaller pieces.

Wrong method or direction of heating: if the solder constantly jumps to one side, or melts in the wrong place, it could be that the heat has been concentrated on one side; the solder naturally moves to the thin side of a piece, even though you are moving the flame from side to side. Therefore concentrate the heat on the bulkier side.

Metal is not the only material which takes heat away from the join and makes heating a lengthy process. A flat piece of metal lying on the charcoal block will take much longer to heat than a piece of similar area which has only a small part in contact with the charcoal or asbestos block. This is because in the first case the charcoal is conducting more heat away from the metal. As you become more confident at soldering, it is a considerable advantage to hold the piece to be soldered in soldering tweezers thus eliminating heat loss.

Overheating is also a hazard. Too intense or too fast heating can cause the solder, especially silver solder, to burn instead of melt. If the surface of the metal begins to shine, it is about to melt. Remove the flame *immediately*. Small pieces are clearly much more liable to melt.

Soldering

Having described the basic principles of soldering and some of the difficulties, I shall finish this chapter by describing two particular methods of using the technique.

Soldering together a piece made up of many small parts, obviously presents difficulties. Unless the parts are supported and soldered together in two or three heatings only, they will collapse and some will probably be melted in the frequent heating. The solution is to build the work piece on some plasticine first (**24, 1**). Then, when you are satisfied with the arrangement, cover it with plaster of Paris, mixed to the consistency of double cream (**24, 2**). Leave the plaster to dry for about 20 minutes. When it is dry, lift the plaster

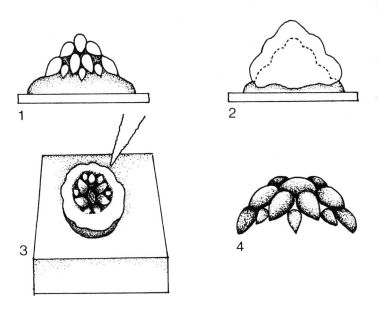

24 Soldering in a plaster of Paris mould

and remove the plasticine: the metal pieces will be embedded in the plaster. Remove all traces of plasticine with petrol or lighter fuel. Borax the metal and lay solder paillons over each join with the borax brush. Play the flame on the outside of the plaster until it becomes red hot (**24, 3**). Then direct the flame on the metal, keeping it moving gently all the time. When the solder has melted, check how many joins it has made, and place new paillons where the original ones have jumped or melted in the wrong place, then reheat the piece. Continue to do this until all the joins have been soldered, or until the plaster cracks and the solder no longer runs easily. If all the joins have not been soldered, replace the piece on the plasticine and repeat the process. When the soldering is completed, remove the plaster (**24, 4**).

The second method, known as 'bringing on', is used when gold or silver soldering are unsuitable because of the high temperatures they require; it is used for example to make a piece set with stones where the stones have to be set before the piece is finally assembled, perhaps because they become inaccessible after the final assembly. The solution to the problem is to solder two or three small tubes to one part (**25, 1**), and pegs, which

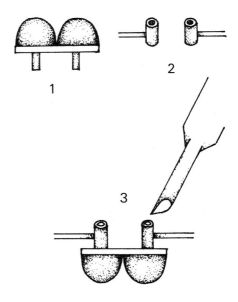

25 Soft soldering two units together (bringing on)

fit tightly into the corresponding tubes, to the other part (**25, 2**). The stones are then set and the final assembly is made by fitting the pegs into the tubes and soldering them in place with soft or lead solder and a soldering iron (**25, 3**).

6 Repoussé & forging

This chapter covers the methods of shaping metal by bending it with pliers or hammering it. First the use of pliers for making rings and stone settings is described, then the repoussé method of raising a design in metal and lastly the shaping or forging of metal by beating it over a metal stake.

The main use of the half round pliers is for bending up curved shapes, the most usual being rings and settings for stones known as collets. These are pieces which you will probably make frequently so although it seems difficult to start with, it is worth persevering until you can turn up a shape accurately because at the same time you will learn to do it quickly. As with all jewellery techniques, practice and a systematic approach produce the most successful results.

Always use half round pliers for bending up a curve; flat pliers mark the inside of the curve, and round ones mark the outside. Round nosed pliers are used for turning up tiny collets of a small number of tiny links or rings, whilst flat nosed pliers are for turning up angles, for example in square or rectangular collets.

To bend up a circle, always start with annealed metal. Hold the strip of metal firmly in the pliers at right angles to them; hold the pliers firmly, do not grip

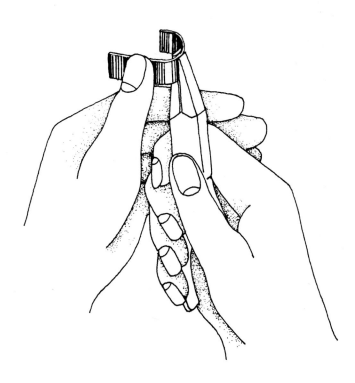

26 Bending up a ring with half round pliers

them so tightly that they dent the metal. Starting with one end of the strip held in the pliers, if you are right-handed and therefore holding the pliers in your right hand, apply pressure to the metal with the thumb of your left hand, about half an inch from the pliers (**26**). This will start the curve. Then move the metal round, about the same distance as the width of the nose of the pliers, and again apply pressure with your left thumb about half an inch from the pliers. Continue to do this, moving the pliers an equal distance each time, and keeping the thumb pressure regular, so that you produce an even curve. As you turn up the ring, check that the strip is forming a vertical wall to the circle, not a slanted one, which can easily happen. If the slant is allowed to continue, you will end up with a spiral, instead of a ring (**27**, left). To correct it, turn the metal the other way up in the pliers, so that the edge which is slanting away from the circle centre is nearest the hinge of the pliers. Hold the ring firmly in your left hand, and ease the strip back into line, then continue to bend up the circle. When the circle is complete, continue to bend the strip, so that it overlaps. This is done because it is diffi-cult to curve the first $\frac{1}{8}$in; it tends to remain resolutely straight, so cut through the two layers of overlapping

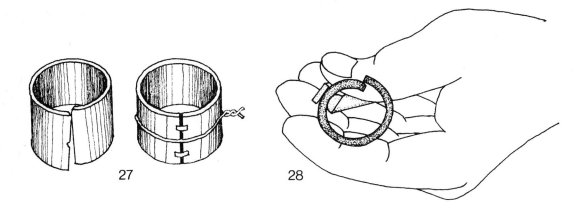

27 Left: spiralled ring;
Right: ring ready for soldering

28 Making a sprung join

metal, where the curve begins, to make a good join. To make a tight join, the metal is sprung into place. In the case of a ring, hold the metal with the half round pliers, a quarter to a third of the circumference away from the join and apply pressure the same distance from the other end with the left thumb, so that the two ends just overlap each other (28), then with the pliers held in the same position pull the outside overlap back and in towards the centre of the circle, so that it meets the other end forming a tightly sprung join. This is done with a twist of the wrist. Check that the join matches from all directions, adjust it if necessary, and solder it (27, right).

Although small collets of thin gauge metal can be shaped with the pliers, until they fit the stone, perfectly shaped large collets or rings are difficult to achieve with pliers only. Circles are particularly difficult to perfect without an additional aid. The conical triblet is made for the purpose of trueing up rings. Place the soldered ring on the triblet, and beat it evenly with the hide or wooden mallet (29). Strike the centre of the ring, not the edges, and rotate the triblet, so that the whole circumference of the ring is treated equally. Having beaten the ring all the way round, remove it from the

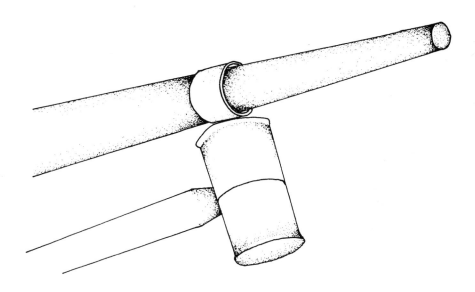

29 Turning up a ring on the triblet

triblet and return it the other way up, then beat it again in the same way. This is done to prevent the ring from taking on the conical shape of the triblet. Hold the triblet up to the light from time to time, to see where daylight shows between the ring and the triblet; where there is a bump which is allowing light through, beat the metal down. It is important to beat the ring in the centre, not at the edges, because the edges would distort. A mallet is used, not a metal hammer, because a soft metal such as gold or silver stretches if it is beaten with a steel hammer against a steel support, whereas hide or wood, being softer than the metals used in jewellery only alters the shape, without stretching the piece. A collet plate and collet punch are available for trueing up conical collets, their use is described in more detail in Chapter 7 below.

For rings, use any gauge metal between BMG 8 and 14. If you want to use thicker gauge metal, the ring has to be beaten, rather than bent into shape; the method is described in the forging section, later in this chapter.

The average length of metal to allow for silver rings is $2\frac{1}{2}$in. This usually gives an adequate overlap. But when using gold it is wise to measure exactly the length required for your finger size, because gold is too expensive to waste. The gauge for stone collets varies according to the size of the stone and the type of collet; this is treated in more detail in Chapter 7.

Repoussé is a decorative method which produces a three-dimensional effect. Three-dimensional effects are particularly difficult to visualize, so if you wish to experiment with your design before committing yourself to gold or silver, or before investing a lot of time in a work piece, you can do so with a very simple form of repoussé work. For this method you need: a sheet of paper-thin metal, BMG 1 or 2 (copper is suitable for the purpose); two or three newspapers to form a support, and two styluses, one $\frac{1}{16}$ to $\frac{1}{8}$in diameter, and the other $\frac{1}{4}$in diameter. To make the styluses, round the ends of two nails or wooden dowels; the metal is so thin, that any hard material can be used. Round the ends with a file, then smooth them with 3/0 emery paper. Place the metal on the thick pad of newspaper, draw the design on to the metal, and then raise the outline with the fine stylus. Use the thick stylus to raise large areas.

To get the feel of the metal, first try geometric designs, using straight lines. Work the fine stylus up and down each line, until you have reached the depth you want. From time to time, turn the work to check the depth and smoothness of the lines being raised on the right side. The materials are so inexpensive that you can afford to make mistakes in the interest of learning.

In the past, repoussé, being a form of sculpture, has lent itself to the most elaborate representational designs. And although contemporary taste does not favour depicting for example, an entire Greek myth in raised silver, it still remains true that figurative designs are well suited to repoussé work. So I suggest experimenting with designs using stylized fish, birds, flowers or leaves.

The simple form of repoussé already described need not be used exclusively for experimental purposes, it can be made into simple jewellery. When the pattern has been raised, cut out the piece with shears or scissors, leaving a border of $\frac{1}{8}$in to $\frac{1}{4}$in round the repoussé. If the piece is square or rectangular, the corners should be rounded. The border is turned in to give the piece more stability and a more finished appearance. Hold the metal at an angle of about 45° to the paper support, with one edge resting on the paper (**30**, left). Then draw the big stylus along just inside the edge, so that a rounded wall is formed perpendicular to the repoussé plate. Turn up this wall all the way round the piece, applying a lot of pressure to corners which will tend to wrinkle. Because the metal is so thin, it has

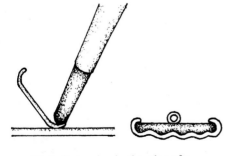

30 Left: turning in the edge of a repoussé piece;
Right: the back is fitted

to be supported in some way to prevent it from being crushed in normal use. To do this, fill the raised parts with plaster of Paris, setting cement, or lacquer. To make a simple brooch, or button, fill the raised piece to just below the top of the turned in edge. Out of a thicker sheet of metal, cut a piece which will fit the back of the repoussé work-piece exactly, and to this piece, solder a brooch pin or a jump ring. Then put it in position, resting on the plaster of Paris and turn the edges of the repoussé piece over to keep it in place (**30**, right).

Repoussé

Real repoussé or a design raised in sheet metal is done with a chasing hammer, punches and a pitch block. The design is then chased, or sharpened on the right side with chasing tools. Directions for making a pitch block were given in Chapter 2. Very simple work can be supported on a lead block, which was also described in Chapter 2. If you use a pitch bowl, or a round enamel bowl, support it on a leather collar. A leather collar is a circle of thick leather which will allow you to tilt the bowl in any direction as you work on it. It is important that the pitch block is heavy so that it does not slide around as you use it. If it does slide, a damp cloth placed underneath it will make some improvement.

Anneal the metal, which should be rectangular, regardless of the proposed shape of the finished piece. Heat the surface of the pitch until it melts, keeping the flame moving all the time so that it does not burn. If it does catch fire, blow out the flames immediately to prevent hard black cinders forming. Remove any which do form. Press the annealed metal down on the soft pitch, making sure that all the lower surface of the metal is supported. Smooth down the pitch which overflows round the edges of the metal. The pitch must cool and solidify completely before any work is done on the metal. Either leave it for half an hour to cool, or run cold water over it for about ten minutes. If the pitch is still soft when you begin to work on it, the metal will sink into it. Either mark the design on the metal before setting it onto the pitch, or trace and scribe it on when the plate is in place. The design must outline the parts to be raised. Start by raising the outlines on what will be the back of the piece with a tracer punch, a narrow straight punch for straight lines, and a narrow curved one for curved lines. Hold the punch in your left hand, tilted slightly away from you, and let it rest on the scribed line. The edge of your hand rests on the pitch block to give you control. Whilst tapping the punch

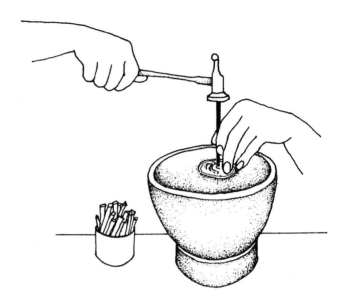

evenly with the chasing hammer, move it slowly towards yourself. The hammer blows should be light, and the movement of the tracer should be smooth and continuous. Irregular heavy blows will produce a bumpy effect. Turn the block so that the punch is always moving towards you, though of course this is not possible when raising a curved line.

Having outlined the design with a tracer, remove the piece by warming the pitch and prising it off. Clean the pitch off the metal with paraffin and check that the lines are sufficiently raised. If they are irregular or unclear, anneal the metal, return it to the pitch, and retrace the lines. If they are satisfactory, replace the piece on the pitch with the raised line on top. The surface you will now work on will be the back of the finished piece. Take a large punch with a round or oval head, and raise the areas which have been outlined (**31**). The depth of the raised work depends on the shape of the punches and the amount of times they are hammered. A slightly curved punch will not create as deep an impression as one which has a more rounded head. Work round the outlined areas systematically. If for example you are raising a long leaf shape, either raise a line down the centre, and then work outwards with lines on either side of the central one, or work round the edges, inside the outline and move gradually to the centre. Remove the metal and anneal it frequently. This makes the metal easier to mould; if you do not anneal the metal frequently, it will become brittle and may crack. Also, removing the metal from the pitch gives you an opportunity to look at the other surface, and if necessary, correct it from the working side. When you have created hollows in the surface, it is important to support them by filling them with pitch before resetting the plate on the pitch block. When the repoussé is complete, the top surface is sharpened with a chasing tool: the work is placed right-side-up in the pitch, and the outline retraced with a chasing tool. Having finished the chasing and repoussé work, cut round the outline if it is not rectangular, and pierce out any open parts in the design. File the edges true, and the piece is ready to be used in whatever context you have selected. For example, as a pendant or part of a pendant, for links in a bracelet, a brooch set with stones, the top of a ring or earrings.

For simple repoussé, for example when you wish to dome a shape, instead of using pitch, a lead block will suffice as support. Grooves can also be made on a lead block. For doming a piece, a set of round headed doming punches is useful, though a punch made by filing a curve on one end of a steel rod can also be used. Anneal the metal, place it on the flat surface of the lead block and using the punch and chasing hammer, beat it regularly. Anneal it again when the metal becomes hard. But before annealing it, carefully clean the surface which has been in contact with the lead with emery. This is because lead has a destructive effect on silver or gold. When it is heated with either, it eats into the metal like acid. Alternatively, you can place a piece of paper between the silver and the lead to prevent any contact.

To make a groove, take a rod with the profile you wish the groove to be; for example if you want to make a right-angled groove, you need a square rod. First make a groove in the lead with the rod, using a corner of the rod to form the bottom of the groove. Then place the metal over the groove, and resting the corner of the rod along the metal, beat the rod, so that it drives the metal into the mould made in the lead.

When the lead block has been used a lot, the surface is covered with depressions. These can be beaten down with a large hammer, but a better surface results from reheating the lead till it is molten.

Domes can also be made in the lead block with a doming punch. Select a doming punch of the required

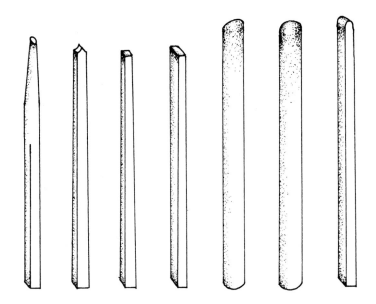

size and hammer it into the lead block, forming a hemispherical depression. Cut out a circle from BMG 6 to 12 depending on the size of the dome, and lay it over the concavity. Place the doming punch over it and beat it into the depression, thus forming a dome. The edges of the dome will need to be filed tidy.

A brass or steel doming block, made specifically for use with doming punches, for making domes, produces better results than a lead block. When using a doming block, first place the flat circle in one of the larger depressions, and beat it with a hammer and a large doming punch. Then anneal it, place it in the depression one size smaller and repeat the process until the dome is the shape you require, or until it will not fit into a smaller hole. Make sure that the metal is beaten thoroughly into the dome, so that the surface of the dome is everywhere in contact with the doming block.

The domes can be soldered to a surface as decoration, or together to form beads.

Forging

Forging includes beating metal into shape over a rounded stake, for example shaping a bangle round a steel mandril; it also includes spreading the metal by beating with a steel hammer or against a steel support, for example beating out the end of a length of wire to form a spatula shape.

Bending up rings from thin gauge metal has already been described in this chapter and it was mentioned that thick gauge metal, that is BMG 16 and over, has to be beaten round a mandril to form a ring. To do this, place the triblet horizontally in the vice, protecting the triblet from the steel jaws of the vice either with copper or rubber jaws, or a pad of cardboard. Anneal the metal, and beat it into a circle, by first beating the ends, and then the centre section over the triblet, with a hide or wooden mallet. If the metal is too thick to be bent with a mallet, use a ballpein hammer and be careful not to strike and mark the triblet. Bangles can be formed in the same way round a bracelet mandril, although being expensive, these are not often used. A cylinder of hard wood approximately $2\frac{1}{2}$in diameter provides a reasonable alternative; a tin can packed with reinforcing material such as sand is another possible alternative.

To turn up a round bangle, measure the circumference of the former or mandril, and use a strip of metal fractionally longer, to account for the thickness of the metal. A circular bracelet with an inside diameter of $2\frac{1}{2}$in can be comfortably fitted over the average woman's hand. Beat the metal round the former and solder the join. A bracelet mandril is oval in section, because the wrist itself is an oval shape. Oval bracelets can also be made on a round mandril. If the oval bracelet is to have a hinge and clasp, the circular mandril it is originally formed on should be less than $2\frac{1}{2}$in in diameter. A diameter of 2in should suffice, but the best method of deciding the diameter is to measure your wrist with a piece of paper, and decide how tight you wish the finished bracelet to be. Turn up a circle the desired diameter and solder it together. At this stage the edges should be filed true. Then stand it on a flat surface, so that the join is exactly midway between the apex and the point where the circle touches the surface. The join will form part of the hinge joint. Holding the bracelet steady with one hand, strike the top in the centre of the strip with the hide mallet. This will begin the transformation from round to oval. Continue to beat it until it forms an even oval, which should not require much hammering. Directions for making a hinge and clasp for a rigid oval bracelet are given in Chapter 9.

There is another way of making an oval bracelet round a former, using $\frac{1}{8}$in square wire and thin gauge sheet, BMG 6 to 10. To make the former, from a flat

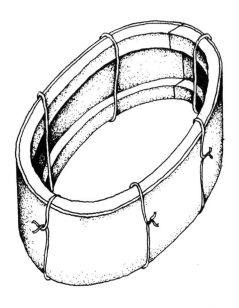

33 Square wire frame bracelet wired together ready for soldering

sheet of thick brass BMG 24/28 about $\frac{1}{8}$in thick, cut an oval the shape and size of the bracelet and file the edges smooth. Then bend the $\frac{1}{8}$in square wire round the former, making the join in the middle of the short side. Make a second identical band, with the join in the same place. When they have been soldered up they may require to be trued up again on the former with a hide mallet, also make sure that they will lie flat on a flat surface.

Next cut a strip of fine gauge metal BMG 6 or 8, which will form the outer wall of the bracelet. It should be as wide as you wish the bangle to be and long enough to be wrapped round the bands. It can be decorated with repoussé patterns. Anneal the strip and wrap it round the two bands, securing it in place with binding wire. Arrange the join in line with the joins of the square wire bands. When the seam between the wire and the strip is touching and secured all the way round, solder the seams (**33**). Directions for a hinge and clasp for this bracelet are also given in Chapter 9.

The method of spreading or stretching a piece of metal by beating it with steel on steel is chiefly used for decorative purposes. Flat or rounded stakes can be used; they should always be kept clean with fine emery

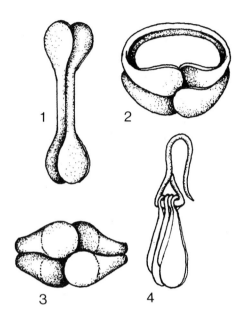

34 Forged ring and ear-ring
1 Both parts of the ring assembled flat
2 Bent round to form the ring
3 Front view of the overlapping discs
4 Ear-ring with four forged pendants

paper. The metal being worked must be frequently annealed to soften it and to prevent it from cracking.

Simple forged work can be most effective and it is useful to get the feel of the metal and some measure of what it will do whilst making very simple work. A simple forged ring can be made with two 2in lengths of thick gauge wire SWG 14–10. Beat out the ends of both strips into rough circles. Lay both pieces on the charcoal, so that the circles of one piece overlap those of the other by about $\frac{1}{8}$in, or so that one side overlaps one end and the other side overlaps at the other (**34, 1**). To make the latter arrangement, it may be necessary to twist the wire fractionally so that both ends can lie flat. Borax and solder the circles, then pickle the piece. Squeeze the two round wires together at the centre, so that they touch. Then solder them together where they touch. Bend the piece round to form a ring and tap it true on the triblet (**34, 2**). To complete the ring you can either overlap the circles and solder them or leave a gap between them (**34, 3**).

To make a pair of forged ear-rings, take a length of wire SWG 20–26, and cut off eight pieces of various lengths between 1in and $\frac{3}{4}$in long. Anneal all the pieces before beating them. On each length of wire, leave $\frac{1}{4}$in

71

unbeaten at one end, which will later be bent into a ring. Working towards the other end, beat the wire regularly, so that it forms a flat spatula shape. Beat the wire more frequently as you work along it, to make the end the widest part. Having beaten all the wires in the same way, bend the unbeaten ends into small rings with the round nosed pliers. Cut off two lengths of SWG 20 wire 2½in long, and with the flat pliers bend up a triangle at one end of each length, each side of which is just over ¼in long. Bend the projecting length of wire so that it is perpendicular to the base line of the triangle. Then solder the join where the short side meets the projecting wire. File a blunt point on the end of the wire and with the half round pliers bend the long piece of wire into an ear hook. Finally attach four of the beaten wires to each of the triangles, by easing open the rings sideways, slipping them on to the base of the triangle, and closing them again (**34, 4**).

Chain links of many different shapes and designs can be beaten out using this method; suggestions for just a few are given here. Cut several short lengths of round or square wire, for example ¾in lengths of SWG 14 or 12; beat out both ends into circular or spatula shapes, then drill a hole at either end to take the joining link. Use the same idea with square wire and after beating out the ends, twist the central wire part of the link three or four times. To make forged circular links, turn up a spiral of rings in SWG 14, cut off the individual rings and join them with solder (see Chapter 8, below). Lay each ring on the flattening stake, and with a ballpein hammer beat two flats opposite each other on the circumference of the ring. Beat each side equally to avoid distorting the whole ring. Link the rings together with links passed through them. The same principle can clearly be used for oval, square or rectangular links.

Cut several ¾in lengths of ⅛in square wire and beat one end of each flat, then turn the wire through a quarter turn so that the beaten end which was horizontal is now vertical, and beat the other end flat. Drill both ends to receive links.

To make the illustrated pendant, first cut out the leaf from BMG 14 sheet metal (**35, 1**). Complex repoussé patterns should be made on rectangular sheets of metal and the outline cut out when the design has been raised but when a whole shape is to be domed, the outline should be cut out first.

The original of this pendant measured 1¾in × 1½in. File up the edge and anneal the piece. Either a lead block or a pitch block can be used as a support. In the case of a lead block, make sure that the surface is level

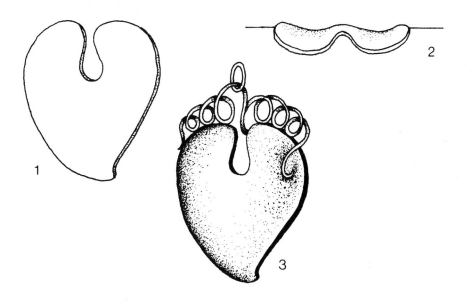

before starting. Fix the leaf on the lead block or the pitch block, and with a large doming punch or shallow curved punch and a hammer, start to beat the centre of the lower part of the leaf. Start in the centre and work gradually outwards with a circular motion, as if you were tracing the form of a snail's shell. Then dome up the two shoulders and work down each side of the pierced out area, to merge the domed shoulders with the rest of the raised area (**35, 2**). When the whole piece has been partially raised and the centre is the highest part, work the punch all the way round the edge of the metal, keeping the punch within the outline. If the punch strikes the edge itself, it will distort it. Lift the leaf and anneal it frequently. Continue to raise it with large punches until the right side is a smooth curved surface. The right side should not need much finishing with files and emery; a fine emery on an emery stick should suffice.

The spirals are part of the design, but they also perform the practical function of providing a loop through which a chain can be threaded. To make them, take a length of SWG wire and wrap it round a mandril or dowel as described in Chapter 8. The mandril should be between $\frac{1}{8}$in and $\frac{1}{4}$in in diameter, and the resulting

73

spiral should be no less than 15 links long. Slip it off the mandril and pull open one end, so that five or six links are extended, twist the extended end, so that the end loops become smaller. Cut off the extended links and solder one end to the back of the leaf between the two shoulders. Then bend the wire with your fingers, so that it forms a loop above the centre of the leaf, and then follows the edge of one of the shoulders. Bring the free end over the surface of the leaf and fix it in place with solder. Arrange the rest of the spiral on the other shoulder to balance the first piece, bending it and soldering it to the leaf in the same way (**35, 3**).

To make a repoussé ring, cut a square of metal $\frac{7}{8}$in × $\frac{7}{8}$in from **BMG** 8 or 10. On it mark a circle $\frac{3}{4}$in diameter. Within the circle mark a cross, the arms of which are $\frac{5}{8}$in long and between the arms of the cross mark eight petal-like shapes, two in each quarter. Fix the metal into the pitch block, design side up. The design is so simple that it is not necessary to outline it first with a tracer. Instead, take a small doming punch, or a punch with straight sides and curved end, and raise the central cross, being careful to keep the lines straight. The best tool to raise the eight 'petals' is a punch exactly the same shape and size as the finished petals (**36, 1**). When the pattern is raised clearly on the right side, clean it with fine emery paper grade 0 and 2/0. Then cut round the scribed circle and file the edge true. To make the setting for the repoussé plate, cut a strip of BMG 10, $\frac{3}{16}$in wide and turn it up into a ring to fit the plate. Solder the join, and true up the ring on the triblet, checking that it fits the plate. Place the plate right side down on the charcoal, and fit the ring over it, then borax and solder the join inside the ring. By soldering from the inside of the ring, you will avoid excess solder spoiling the right side of the piece. Check that the solder has run all the way round the seam, and fill in any gaps if it has not. Then stand the piece on a sheet of BMG 8, and solder it to the sheet (**36, 2**). Then cut the sheet metal away round the setting, file it flush with the setting and remove the file marks with emery paper grades 3 and 0.

From BMG 12 or 14 turn up a ring $\frac{1}{4}$in wide, to fit your finger size. Solder the join and true it up on the triblet. Round the edges with a file, and finish it with a file if it is badly marked, and then emery paper of the same grades as before. Now the ring is ready to be joined to the top part. Solder alone would not join them adequately, so in addition to the solder, a peg which passes through the ring and the base of the top part should be used. Take a piece of round wire SWG 20, and a drill of exactly the same diameter. With the dividers mark a point exactly in the middle of the width of the ring opposite the join. Make the mark a deeper indentation with the scriber, or a sharp pointed instrument. Make a similar mark in the centre of the base of the top piece. One way of finding the centre is to draw a circle of the same diameter with compasses on a piece of paper. Cut out the circle, lay it on the base and mark the centre through the paper. Hold the ring in a hand vice or the engineer's vice with the marked point uppermost. Place the tip of the drill in the marked point and holding the drill vertical, make a hole through the ring. Place the repoussé piece upside down on the bench and drill the marked point in the same way. The recess prevents the drill from slipping over the metal. File a small facet on the outside of the ring over the drilled hole, so that the hole is in the centre of the facet. This provides a larger area of contact for the solder between the two parts of the piece.

To make the peg, cut off a piece of wire long enough to go through the ring and into the top part with a little excess projecting from the hole in the ring. Push it into place so that both parts are held tightly together, bind them together with binding wire if necessary (**36, 3**).

Place the piece on the charcoal so that it rests on the repoussé plate. Borax the join between the two units and where the wire projects inside the ring. Put paillons of soft solder in both places and heat the whole piece gently. The solder should run along the peg, holding it in place in both drilled holes; it should also cover the area of contact between the two parts. Pickle the ring, file off any excess solder and finally polish it (**36, 4**).

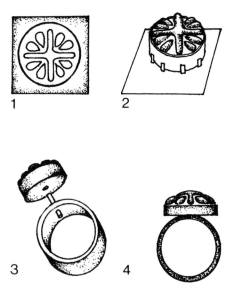

36 Repoussé ring
1 Design marked out on sheet metal
2 Raised design cut out and soldered into a round bezel now prepared for soldering on to a flat base
3 Top and ring shank are pegged as well as soldered together
4 The finished ring

7 Stone setting

This chapter describes the different types of setting suitable for the different types and cuts of stones described in Chapter 3. Basically the different settings are as follows: *Rub over settings*, most suitable for cabochon and opaque stones, and also for brittle stones such as emeralds or opals. However, faceted stones can also be set in this way. These settings obviously do not allow in as much light as claw settings; for this reason they tend to darken and in some cases improve the colour of a faceted stone. They are made with a solid or open back. A clear cabochon stone such as a garnet or a moonstone is enhanced by an open backed setting because of the light passing through the stone. A turquoise should be set with a solid backing, because it is a delicate stone, which should be protected as far as possible from moisture or heat, and being opaque, gains nothing from the passage of light. *Claw settings* are used for faceted gemstones. They allow the maximum amount of light to reach the stone, thus exploiting the refractive and reflective properties of the stone. There are two types of claw setting. One is cut out of solid metal, whilst the other is constructed with wire. Each stone shape will demand slightly different treatment. *Gypsy settings* are used for flat stones with chamfered edges, such as signet stones. They are a variation on the rub over setting.

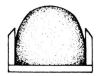

37 Left: sufficient setting edge for a cabochon stone
Right: insufficient setting edge

A band ring with a rub over set cabochon stone

Make a band ring, as explained in Chapter 5. Then, to make a rub over setting for a round stone, measure the diameter of the stone with calipers, and calculate the length of the strip of metal required by multiplying the diameter by three and adding a bit.

Estimate the height of metal needed from the base of the stone to keep the stone in its setting (**37**). (A steep sided stone needs more setting edge than a shallow one.)

Allow enough space below the base of the stone for a bearer wire to support the stone. In this case the setting or bezel is shaped to fit the ring, so enough metal must be allowed for this (**39**). Otherwise, the height of the setting is a question of taste.

Cut a strip of metal to the measurements calculated above; in this case using metal gauge 10. Make sure that the sides are all straight by marking out the metal accurately and filing it true after sawing. Make sure that the ends are straight and at right angles to the long sides. As a guide to the selection of metal gauges for settings, for stones diameter 4 to 15mm use metal gauge 8; for stones diameter 15 to 25mm use metal gauge 10–12. Anneal the strip, taking care not to overheat it. With half round pliers, bend up the strip into a circle, overlapping the ends and bend the metal until it fits the stone (**38, 1**). If necessary, cut off the excess through both layers, so that you have a clean matching joint (**38, 2**). Remember to allow for the thickness of the sawblade. Spring the join together to give a tight join through which no daylight is visible. To spring the join together as explained in Chapter 5, hold the bezel in half round pliers opposite the join. Apply pressure with the thumb of your other hand, so that first you increase the overlap, then bend it open again pressing the inner edge outwards. Solder the join, bound with binding wire if necessary. Heat the whole piece evenly to avoid it springing open, take care not to overheat it.

Check the fit. The stone should sit in the setting with no more than a fraction of daylight visible between the stone and the setting. If it is too large, cut out a piece and resolder. Remember that a circle is reduced considerably by the removal of a small piece from its circumference. If it is slightly too small, place the bezel on a metal cylinder or cone, eg the triblet or the shaft of

1   2   3   4

38 Rub over setting
1 Overlap the ends
2 Cut through both cleanly
3 Solder bearer inside the setting
4 Stone in collet ready for setting

a doming tool. Tap the centre of the band evenly, using the centre, not the edge of the hammer. This will stretch the metal. If the bezel is much too small, start again; it saves time in the end. The stone needs a bearer on which to rest. In the case of a setting for a brooch or ear-rings this can be a base plate. Solder the bezel to a thin sheet of metal and cut round the bezel. For this ring a bearer wire is most suitable. Bend up a piece of wire to fit the inside of the bezel. Solder it and tap it flat, then solder it inside the bezel (**38, 3**). It is important that the bearer wire fits properly inside the bezel: if it is soldered in at an angle, the stone will be too (**38, 4**).

The metal will be too thick to push over the stone, so the setting edge must now be filed thinner. The top of the setting should be true, so taking it as a guide line, mark a parallel line 4mm below with calipers. File the metal thinner to this line (**39, 2**). Don't take too much metal off the top edge as this will result in the setting edge splitting and flaking. It is an easy mistake to make. For a setting of this size use the ring file Cut 2 initially, then finish with a finer file and emery paper. File evenly all the way round the setting, taking off the same amount all the way round. Don't concentrate on one area because this will result in an uneven, bumpy

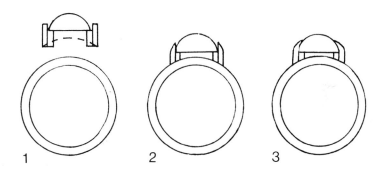

39 Rub over setting
1 File a curve in the setting to fit the ring
2 File the setting edge
3 The tapered setting edge pushed over the stone

effect. Then with the half round file, file two curves opposite each other on the base of the bezel, to fit the curve of the shank. Keep the curve in the centre of the frame. Marking the centre on both sides and the points equidistant from the centre helps you to keep the curve in place and regular. File, first from one side and then the other, checking all the time (**39, 1**).

When you have cleaned and polished the ring, it is ready for the stone.

To set the stone, place it in the setting and gently work the metal over the stone with a burnisher, or initially with a copper pusher (**39, 3; 40**). If the metal does not move easily or lies in bumps round the stone or does not hold the stone still, file the setting edge thinner with a needle file. Remove scratches from the setting edge with water of Ayr stone if necessary and burnish with a burnisher.

The agate in the silver and agate ring is set in a slightly different way. The fine setting edge is soldered into an outer bezel instead of being filed down. To make this ring you need a strip of BMG 6, $2 \times \frac{1}{8}$in for the setting edge; a strip of BMG 12, $\frac{3}{8} \times 3\frac{1}{2}$in for the outer bezel and shank; SWG 20 square wire $2\frac{1}{2}$in long for the bearer.

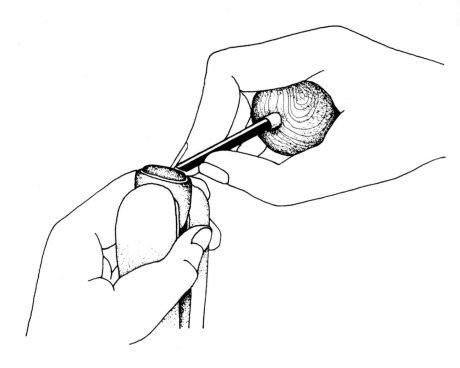

40 Stone setting: the ring held in the ring clamp and the setting edge pushed over the stone with a copper pusher

First make the setting for the stone using the BMG 6 strip. With the half round pliers bend up a collet which fits the stone, and solder it together with medium solder. Bend up the square wire to form a bearer, which fits inside the collet and solder it in place (**41, 1**). Next, bend up the outer frame to fit round the setting edge, solder it together with medium solder, and check that the sides are parallel (**41, 2**). Then, with the half round file, file a curve in one side of the outer frame. This will form part of the shank round the finger (**41, 3**). Stop filing when the metal between the two arches is the right width to make a good shoulder to the shank. With the dividers, measure the width of the shoulders, adding a bit to allow for the curve; this is the width of the shank which you cut from the remaining piece of BMG 12 sheet. To assess the length of strip needed for the shank, place the top frame on your finger, or on the triblet at the point where it matches the required finger size, and measure the length needed with a piece of stiff paper. The shank is not the same width all the way round, so cut an identical curve out of both sides, as shown in the illustration (**41, 4**). With the half round pliers, bend the wedge shaped ends to fit the curve of the top frame (**41, 5**), then bend round the whole shank so that both ends meet the top frame. To do this, use the half round

1.   Six gold rings, made with twisted wire or filed out of solid metal.

2.   Amethyst and gold ring; the amethyst is held in a claw setting. Maker: *Alison Richards*. Cast silver shell ear-rings. Maker: *Iain Doxford*. Cast silver sycamore seed ear-rings. Maker: *Iain Doxford*

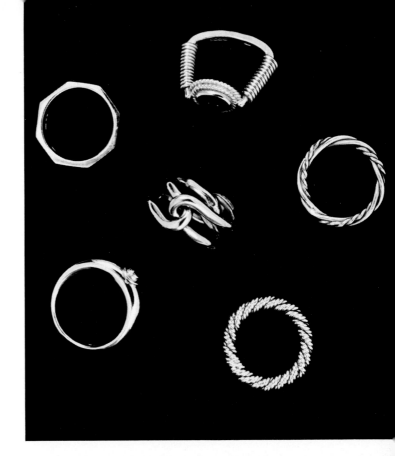

3. Silver bracelet of molten silver wire, onyx, ivory, shell and agate beads. Maker: *Hamish Aikman*. Ivory, amber and silver pendant. The silver leaves are riveted to the cabochon amber. Maker: *Alison Richards*

4. *Left to right:* Silver cufflinks decorated with cut-out clouds applied with solder. Maker: *Judy Keeling*. Silver stars and moonstone ring. Maker: *Judy Keeling*. Molten silver ring decorated with applied wire. Maker: *Marian Watson*. *Centre:* Silver and moss agate ring. Maker: *Alison Richards*

5. Silver monkey ring. Silver mouse ring. Both these rings were modelled in wax, then cast in silver. Maker: *Paula Phillips*

6. Silver box decorated with silver wire and beads, and set with cabochon stones. Maker: *Patti Clarke*

7. Pierced silver bangle.
Maker: *Clive Cooke*

8. Gold and diamond
pendant. Gold, diamond
and ivory heart pendant.
Maker: *Jane Allen*

9. Nickel silver, bright nickel and black chrome plate bracelet, of which each section is pierced out separately. Maker: *Gillian Gregory*

10. Silver butterfly bangle. The butterfly is inlaid with copper and steel. Maker: *Richard Anderson*

11. Six silver rings set with stones in rub-over settings.
Maker: *Gerda Flockinger*

12. Four silver rings set with pearls and cabochon stones in
rub-over settings, and a bracelet set with cabochon stones.
All the rings have been modelled in wax and cast. Maker:
Sue Cohen

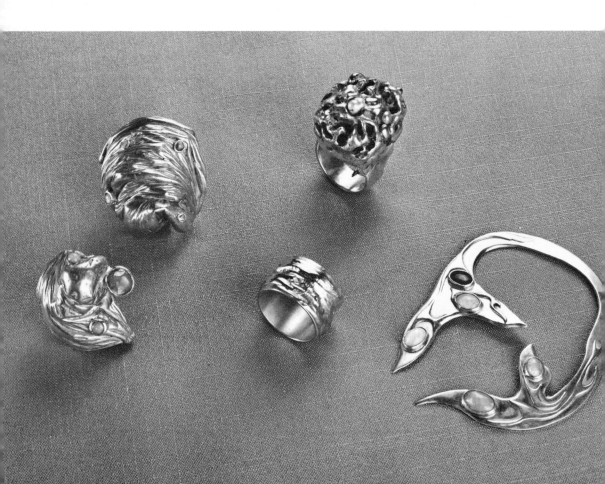

13. Two silver rings cast in silver.
Maker: *Gerda Flockinger*

14. Silver necklace inlaid with
acrylic resins. Maker: *Susanna Heron*

15. Gold, cabochon amethyst and
diamond ring. Each piece is pierced
out separately and soldered
together. Maker: *Alison Richards*

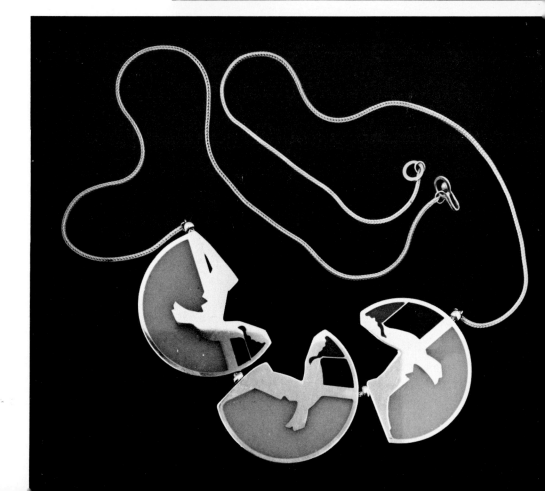

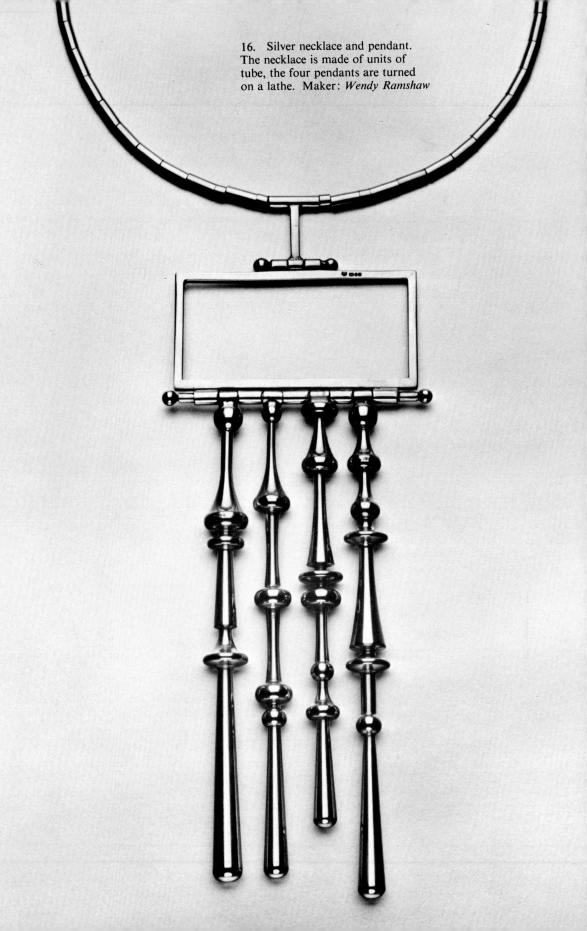

16.   Silver necklace and pendant. The necklace is made of units of tube, the four pendants are turned on a lathe. Maker: *Wendy Ramshaw*

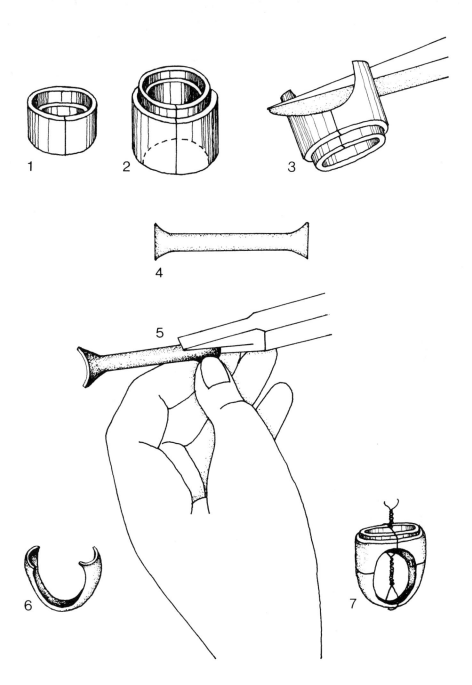

41 Agate and silver ring
1 Collet with bearer
2 Collet soldered into an outer bezel
3 Curve of shank filed
4 The back of the shank
5 Shoulders of the shank curved with half round pliers
6 Shank bent up to fit top bezel
7 Ring wired up ready for soldering

pliers and bend two angles in the shank where it narrows, so that the wedge shaped ends will meet the top frame in a straight line (**41, 6**). Wire the shank and the top frame together, and solder them with medium solder. The join must not have any gaps filled with solder, because the solder will run out during subsequent heating. If it proves difficult to match the shank and the top frame exactly, solder them together with bad joins and saw through one side and resolder it; then saw through the other and resolder it.

Put the ring on the triblet and tap it as near round as possible. Then file off the excess metal which is preventing the shank from being a circle; this will probably be chiefly round the two joins. Having made the ring round, check that the top of the bezel is still flat, and file it true if necessary. Remove any excess solder, and finish the ring as far as the fine emery stage. Next solder in the setting edge and bearer wire with easy solder, leaving the setting edge at least $\frac{1}{16}$ in proud of the outer frame (**41, 7**). Grip the back of the shank in the soldering tweezers, and hold the ring upright. There are two possible hazards to beware of in this operation. The first is that the setting edge, or bearer wire may melt, because these are the smallest areas of metal, so do not concentrate the flame directly on them: the second is that the solder in the shoulder joints may melt, so avoid overheating the piece and hold it upright.

Clean off any excess solder with a flat needle file and water of Ayr stone, then polish the ring. Finally set the stone in the same way as the previous ring and give it one more buff on the polishing mop.

Claw settings

When selecting faceted stones to set, it is worth bearing in mind two factors, one of which has already been mentioned. Stones with big flaws or cracks in them will break more easily during the setting process than unflawed stones, whilst stones with big bellies are the most difficult to set.

Wire settings

This is the simplest way of making claw settings, best suited to oval or round stones, but usable for square or rectangular ones. They do require a certain assurance with soldering which is obtained with practice.

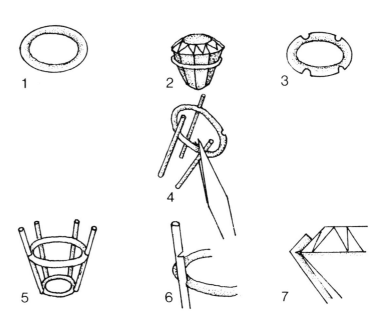

42 Stages of making a wire collet
1 The bezel
2 Bezel round girdle of the stone
3 Bezel notched for the claws
4 Claws soldered to bezel
5 Claws and bezel soldered to collet base.
6 Claw filed to receive stone
7 Claw holding stone

TO SET AN OVAL STONE 8 × 6MM

Turn up a straight piece of annealed round wire, gauge 20 SWG, to fit the stone just below its girdle so that the outside of the wire is in line with the girdle of the stone and the belly of the stone rests on the wire. If the stone is very deep and wide below the girdle, the bezel will come about half way down the stone, but with a shallow stone, there will be less distance between the girdle and the bezel (42, 1, 2). Solder the wire with hard solder, check that the join is perfect; resolder it if it is not and file off any excess solder. Flatten the bezel and check it for fit. If it does not fit, adjust it with half round pliers. If you find difficulty in adjusting the curve of an oval bezel, make it round on the triblet, or on a round rod of suitable size, or with the collet punch. Then squeeze the circle very gently in the parallel pliers; this produces a regular shaped oval which should be easier to adjust to the correct shape. To use the collet punch, first press the short sides of the oval together in parallel pliers, until it is more circular. Then place it over a hole in the collet plate which is just smaller in diameter, put the collet punch through the bezel and tap it gently with the mallet. Make sure the bezel stays flat on the surface

83

of the plate and does not slip into the hole where it will be distorted. Also be careful not to stretch the metal which will easily happen if you hit the collet punch too hard.

Mark four points on the bezel, where you will attach the claws. The combined use of calipers and your own judgement is as effective as painstaking measurement for this operation. With the round needle file, make a groove at each of the four marked points into which the claws will lodge (**42, 3**). The grooves should be at a slanted angle to the bezel, not perpendicular, so that the claws will be at a slanted angle in line with the base of the stone. The maximum depth of the groove should be two-thirds of the bezel wire thickness.

For the claws, take a straight piece of round wire, also 20 SWG, and cut four pieces 15mm long. (The claws are later cut shorter.) A rule of thumb for deciding the length of the claws is to measure the height of the stone and double it – you can always cut off excess metal, but you cannot add any.

The next stage is to solder the claws to the bezel. If the bezel has got marked or scratched, file it clean now, because it will be less accessible once the claws are soldered on. Place the middle of the first claw in its groove and hold it there with tweezers (**42, 4**). Borax it and place a paillon of medium solder on the join. Make sure the claw is at the right angle to the bezel and heat the piece gently until the solder runs. Pickle and rinse it. Repeat this process with the next claw, matching up its angle with the first. The danger is, of course, that while soldering the second claw, you will melt the solder of the first one, and the risk increases as you add the remaining two claws. There is no easy answer to this problem. Keep the flame small and concentrate the heat on the joint you are soldering, keeping it off the other claws. In time you will get the knack.

Put the stone in the collet and mark a point on the claws below the base tip of the stone. Cut off all the claws to this point and file the ends flat with a needle file so that the collet will stand on a flat surface.

Turn up a second oval of 20 SWG wire, which will form the base of the collet; all the claws must fit on to this base. You may have to adjust the angle of the claws slightly with flat pliers. Use a file or emery to make a small flat area on the base so that the collet will stand on it more easily. Place the collet on the base on a charcoal block and solder the claw tips to the base using easy solder (**42, 5**). Again be careful not to melt the claw joints. Alternatively, snip the top ends of the claws even, so that the collet will stand upside down on the charcoal and place the collet base on top to solder

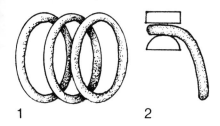

1   2

3

43 Amethyst ring shank
1 Three rings form shank
2 Bending outer ring
3 Rings soldered together

it. This removes the risk of the charcoal conducting away the heat from the base, resulting in the rest of the collet overheating before the base is hot enough to take solder.

Clean up the collet carefully using the half round needle file, Cut 2, to remove excess solder and scratches, then using emery paper Grades 2/0 and 0 or a very fine needle file, eg Cut 6. The collet is now ready to be soldered into a larger piece of jewellery.

To make the illustrated amethyst ring you need a length of SWG 16 wire, and some BMG 10 sheet. Make the collet to fit the stone as described above until you come to solder on the lower bezel or base. This bezel has to be slightly curved to fit the curve of the ring shank, so hold the flat bezel on the triblet and tap it into a shallow curve. Then solder it to the rest of the collet.

To make the shank, turn up three rings from SWG 16 in the finger size you want the finished ring to be (**43, 1**). With the half round pliers, bend a kink in two of them as illustrated (**43, 2**). Solder one of these to the plain ring, holding them in the soldering tweezers, then solder on the other one (**43, 3**). Cut through the centre of the middle ring (**44, 1**), and bend back the two ends, so that the collet fits between them (**44, 2**). Measure the width of the base at the claws and cut this from the two side rings. Bend the ends of the central ring so that they meet the top bezel of the collet. Saw or file off any excess if necessary. The collet should fit so tightly into the gap in the ring that it is held in position. However, it is wise to hold the two together with binding wire, whilst you solder them. Before you solder them, make sure that the ring is annealed and will not spring open during soldering. Do not use too much solder, because this will be difficult to remove afterwards; two small paillons should suffice for each join. Keep the flame away from the claws.

Cut four small leaves out of the BMG 10 sheet and slightly dome them in the doming block with doming punches. To arrange them on each side of the collet, wedge a small piece of plasticene on each shoulder, and lay the leaves on this so that they touch each other at one point at least. Pour a little plaster of Paris over each side, so that when it sets, the leaves are held in two tiny plaster moulds which can be easily removed from the rest of the ring. Remove all traces of the plasticene from the plaster and leaves with petrol or lighter fuel and solder the leaves together. Remove the plaster by dropping it into cold water and pickle the two sets of leaves. Clean off any excess solder; lay them in place on the ring and solder a pair at a time. Clean up and polish the ring which is then ready for the stone to be set.

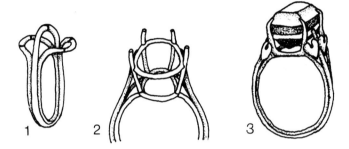

44 Inserting collet in amethyst ring
1 Central ring of shank sawn through
2 Collet fitted into shank
3 Stone set in shank

When the setting stage is reached, secure the piece in setting cement on the end of a wooden dowel, place the stone in the collet and mark where the girdle of the stone rests on the claws. Remove the stone and file or saw a tiny v-shaped notch at the mark you have just made on the claws (**42, 6**). With the thin nosed flat pliers, bend three of the claws inwards from the notch and put the stone in the collet. The girdle of the stone should now be held in the three bent claws. Bend the fourth claw inwards so that it too holds the stone (**42, 7**). This is when it is important to have at least 4mm of claw above the notch to give you leverage. With the saw, carefully cut off the excess from each claw, leaving enough metal to be pushed over the stone. Round off the tip of the claw with a needle file and push it over the stone with the copper pusher. All the claws should rest on the stone so that they will not catch in anything (**44, 3**). Clean up the claws with water of Ayr stone or emery.

The method for making wire collets is basically the same for all other shapes of stones. For a pear shaped stone, turn up a bezel to fit the stone below the girdle, joined anywhere except at the point. Use three claws, one at the point, and the other two on either side of the

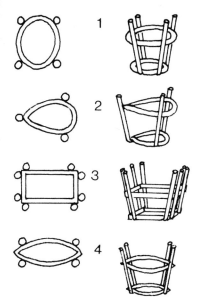

45 Positioning claws for wire collets
1 Oval stone
2 Pear shaped stone
3 Rectangular stone
4 Marquise stone

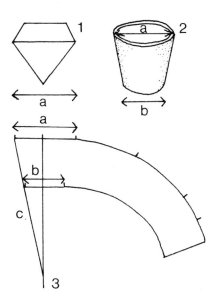

46 Curtain collet: measurements
1 Stone diameter
2 Base diameter of collet
3 Measuring the strip

widest part (**45, 2**). Attach them in the same way as described for the oval collet (**45, 1**). The base bezel should always be the same shape as the upper one. For marquise shaped stones, four claws are advisable, two each end, near the points (**45, 4**). It is possible to use only two, one at each end, but the claws should be relatively thick and there is always a danger of breaking off the tip of the stone during setting. The corners of square or rectangular stones are also vulnerable; it is best to use eight claws, one on either side of each corner (**45, 3**).

To set a rectangular stone, decide how low down the collet the stone should lie, allowing enough metal above the girdle to press over the stone. Mark each claw where the girdle is to be held in place. Cut a small notch with the saw at each mark. Bend out the tops of the claws, so that the stone can rest in the notches. Very gently squeeze in the claws opposite each other, until the stone is held in place, then push the claws over the stone individually with the copper pusher. Cut off any excess with the saw and finish with a burnisher and a file or water of Ayr stone.

A curtain collet is usually used for a round stone; the first step is to make a conical collet. Here you need a curved strip of metal. On a piece of BMG 10 or 12 scribe a line (a) equal in length to the diameter of the stone (**46, 1**). Drop a perpendicular through the centre of that line (**46, 3**). Parallel with line (a) scribe a second line (b) equal in length to the base diameter of the collet (**46, 2**) and bisected by the perpendicular (**46, 3**). The distance between (a) and (b) will be the height of the upper bezel of the final collet and should be at least the distance between the girdle and the culet or pointed 'base' of the stone. Draw a line (c) joining the ends of the parallel lines and continue it until it meets the perpendicular line (**46, 3**). This line (c) gives you the radii (ca) and (cb) of two arcs which you now scribe (**47, 1**). Cut out a length of the strip formed between the two arcs, slightly longer than three times the diameter of the stone. Turn this up into a conical collet with the half round pliers (**47, 2**), and solder the join with hard solder. If necessary, true up the collet with the collet punch and collet plate, and file up the top, base and wall of the collet. Precise measuring and marking out on the collet is essential to the final result. On the top of the collet, mark out the position of the claws and draw a fine saw blade straight across the centre, then at right angles, then half-way between the four marks (**47, 3**). If the collet is very small, secure it with setting cement to the end of a thin dowel rod, so that it can be held firmly and mark six, not eight, claws. Extend the marked lines down either side of the

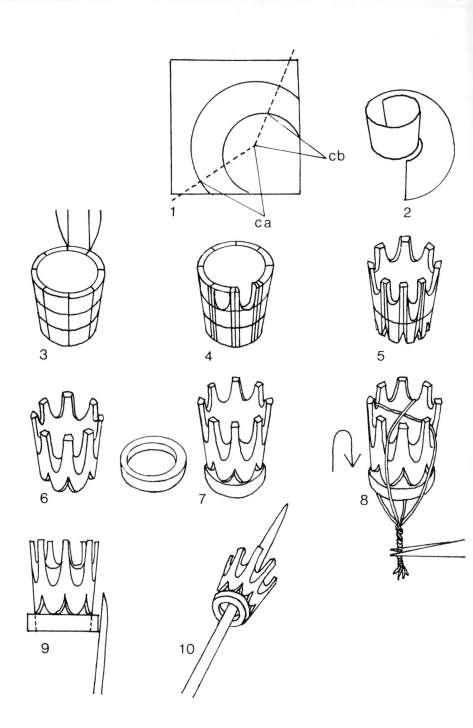

47 Curtain collet: construction
1 Scribing strip for collet
2 Turning up collet
3 Marking claws
4 Filing claws
5 Claws completed and notched
6 Tapered grooves at base
7, 8 Collet soldered to base
9, 10 Base filed into shape

collet and draw a line down either side of each one (**47, 4**). Then draw two lines round the collet, one-third and two-thirds from the top. Cut and file away the metal between the claws as far as the upper line making u-shaped gaps (**47, 5**). Next, file a tapered groove on the outside of the collet down to the lower line, using a round needle file (**47, 5**). With the triangular needle file, make a notch at the base of each claw, then extend the notch to form a curve which echoes the curve between the claws, so that the base of the collet is scalloped with inverted pointed arches (**47, 6**).

To make the lower bezel, either turn up a square-wire circle, if you have a suitable wire gauge or use thick gauge sheet metal. Solder the upper bezel on to the ring or sheet and then drill, saw and file the lower bezel flush (**47, 7–10**). The collet should require very little cleaning, because this should be done at each stage of its construction. It is now ready to be incorporated into a piece of jewellery, where it should be polished before the stone is set in it. To set the stone, place the stone on top of the collet and bend the claws in or out until the girdle rests on about half the thickness of the claws all round. Remove the stone and file away half the thickness of the claws, leaving a ledge for the stone to rest on and enough metal projecting above the girdle to push in or grip with the small flat pliers. With the pliers, turn in two adjacent claws, slip the stone into position and push over the two opposite claws with the copper pusher or the burnisher. Push the remaining claws over the stone and when it is securely held with no trace of rocking, finish them off with the file and the water of Ayr stone.

There are several ways of making collets for square, rectangular and trap cut stones (**48, 1**), but they are all similar and there is only room here to describe one of them. The bezel is made with square wire, the gauge depending on the size of the stone and whether you want a heavy or light looking collet. To make the corners square they have to be mitred. This is done by filing an angle through two-thirds of the thickness of the metal with the triangular file (**48, 2**) and then bending the metal round to form a right angle, using the flat pliers and the parallel pliers (**48, 3**). Secure the angle with hard solder and make the next angle. The outside dimensions of the bezel should be the same as the girdle of the stone, and the join should be in the middle of the long side, not at a corner (**48, 4**). File a bevel on the inside of the collet on which the stone rests. Cut four wedge shaped claws out of BMG 10, about $\frac{3}{32}$in tapering to $\frac{1}{32}$in, and a little longer than the final height of the setting (**48, 5**). Make a right-angle v-shaped

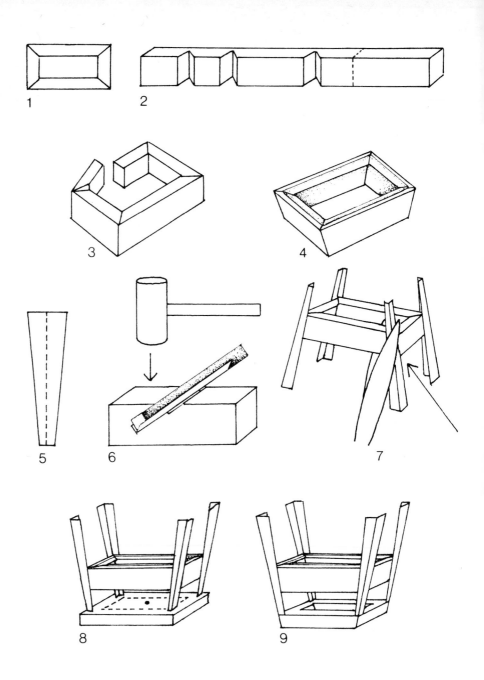

48 Collets for rectangular stones
1 Rectangular stone
2 Collet filed for mitring
3 Collet bent to shape
4 Soldered collet
5 Wedge-shaped claw
6 Claw beaten into shape
7 Claw held for soldering
8 Collet soldered to base
9 Base pierced

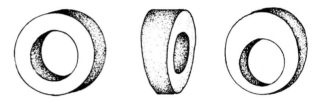

49 Preparing the thick metal ring for a gypsy setting

groove in the lead block with a square rod. Place the claw in this with the square rod on top of it and beat the rod to form a right-angled claw (**48, 6**). On the bezel, mark the position of the claw, and then file a groove so that the claw will be slanted in line with the belly of the stone. Solder on the claws with medium solder (**48, 7**). Check that they are all the same length below the bezel. Then solder the piece on to a base plate of sheet metal (**48, 8**). Cut out the centre of the base and file the outside edge flush with the claws (**48, 9**).

To set the stone, press the claws in until the stone is held in place, then saw off the excess and file the tips thinner so that they can be pushed flat over the stone.

Gypsy setting

For a gypsy setting you need a metal gauge as thick as the height of the stone. Mark the outline of the stone on the metal (**50, 1**) and saw inside that line, making a hole with tapered sides (**50, 2, 4**). If the stone is round, grind out the top of the collet with a conical phrase, leaving a ledge for the stone to rest on (**50, 3, 5**). If the stone is not round, either gouge out a rim with the chisel graver

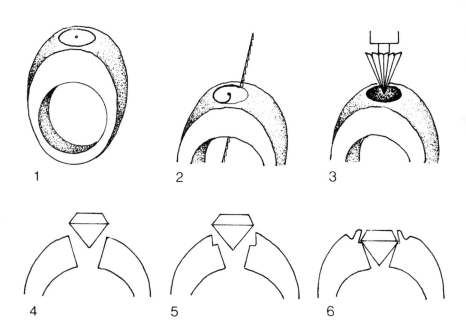

50 Gypsy setting
1 Outline of stone marked
2 Sawing round outline
3 Grinding ledge for stone
4 Section of 2 above
5 Section of 3 above
6 Grooved setting edge

or cut the opening large enough for the stone to drop into it, and solder in a bearer to support the stone. With the round bottomed scorper (see page 124), carve a groove about $\frac{1}{32}$in deep, about $\frac{1}{32}$in from the stone (**50, 6**). This will leave a ridge, which forms the setting edge. Push the metal over the stone, by placing a flat pusher against the edge, and tapping it gently with the jeweller's hammer. This must be done with great care because of the risk of damaging the stone. It is best to use only hard stones such as agates in gypsy settings. When the stone is set, clean up the groove with a scorper and if the stone is set deep enough, clean up the setting with a file and water of Ayr stone. To make a signet ring with a gypsy set stone, you need a strip of metal thick enough to take the gypsy setting. Bend this into a ring, beating it round with a hammer if necessary (**49, 1**). Then file off the excess metal at the back of the shank and round it up (**49, 2**). The ring is then ready for the setting to be cut (**49, 3**).

92

8 Wire work and chains

There are many different ways of using wire decoratively, including twisted rope, chains and filigree. Gold, silver and copper wire can be bought in several shapes; round, square or half round are generally available in several gauges. But laying in a stock of different shapes and gauges of wire is an extravagant way of doing things; the money would be better spent on draw plates. A draw plate is a slab of hardened steel, $\frac{1}{4}$in thick, $1\frac{1}{2}$in high and from 5 to 9in long, drilled with a series of tapered holes, graduated in size. Draw plates are available with round, square, rectangular, triangular, oval, knife edged, pipin or sage shaped holes (**51**). For normal purposes a square hole plate, and a round hole plate ranging in size from 75mm upwards will suffice (**52, 1**).

To draw wire through the draw plate, you need a pair of draw tongs, although a stout pair of pliers with serrated jaws or a mole wrench will do as well. With a file, taper the last inch off one end of the wire, so that it will go through the draw plate (**52, 2**). Let it project far enough the other side to allow you to get a good purchase with the tongs. Fix the draw plate firmly in the bench vice. Anneal the wire, find the smallest hole it will pass through undrawn, and insert the tapered end

1 2 3 4 5 6 7 8

51 Draw plate sections
1 round
2 square
3 rectangular
4 triangular
5 oval
6 knife edged
7 pipin
8 sage

through the next smaller hole from the back of the plate. Grip the tapered end and draw it steadily through (52, 3). To facilitate this process, lubricate the wire with oil. Anneal the wire frequently; about every five or six holes. If it is allowed to become hard, it will be more difficult to pull, and more liable to break. To anneal a long piece of wire, wrap it into a coil, securing the ends by wrapping them round the coil to prevent them from straightening up during heating. Draw the wire in one pull if possible, as each time the pull is interrupted, a small kink is left where the wire may break next time through. It is very useful to measure and record how much a given length of wire will stretch when it is pulled through each hole. With these measurements you can calculate how much wire you will need for any particular job.

The first simple and decorative use of wire is achieved by twisting it. The wire can be twisted by itself, or combined with different gauges and shapes. There are infinite possibilities for different patterns, whilst the technique remains extremely simple. The tools needed for making a short length of twist are the bench vice and a hand vice. A hand drill is very useful if you want to make a lot of twists.

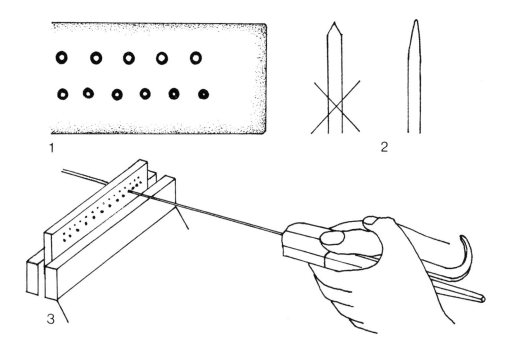

52 Tapering and drawing wire
1 The draw plate
2 Correctly tapered wire comes to a long point
3 Wire drawn through hole in draw plate

To make a simple twist, take a length of annealed wire, fix one end in the vice, the other in the hand vice or the hand drill and twist. If you want a double twist, bend the wire in half, secure the ends in the bench vice and the loop in a hook held in the hand vice or the hand drill (**53**). You can use any shape of wire. Different gauges of flat, square and round can be used in endless different combinations. The spiral of a long twist will tend to be uneven as the part farthest from the hook will be the tightest. To counteract this, hold the tightly twisted part still, with your thumb and index finger, while you twist the loose part. It is important to anneal the wire evenly throughout its length. If some parts are not annealed properly, the twist will be uneven and the wire may break.

A plain double twist and some variations are shown here (**54**); 2 is a double twist of thick wire with a double twist of finer wire wound round it; 3 is a fine double twist wound round a plain twist of flat wire; 4 is a plain twist of flat strip wire; 5 is a tightly wound double twist of thick wire with a thinner wire wound round the groove; 6 is a double twist of thick wire; 7 is another plain twist of flat strip wire, like 4, but it is wound more tightly: 8 is a double twist made of two coloured

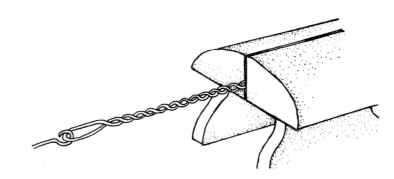

53 Twisting wire

metals; 9 is a tight right-hand twist, doubled back and then twisted tightly in the opposite direction.

The twists can be used in many different ways. It is worthwhile looking at Mexican, Indian or African jewellery for ideas, because twists are an important part of their styles. The twists can be used for applied decoration, for example as frames for stones, or they can be used for making bracelets and rings. In the case of bracelets, bend the annealed twisted wire round and either secure the ends with solder or finish off each end separately with a spherical terminal or a wire binding. Wire is also very decorative when plaited.

Chains

To make chains you need links, which are very easily made. Take a round metal rod, the diameter of which will be the inside diameter of the spring or ring (a straight-sided nail or a knitting needle may be used for this purpose), some tissue paper and a bench vice. A hand vice can be used if rod and wire are very fine.

First damp the paper and wrap it round the rod; then secure the rod and one end of the wire in the vice. Next

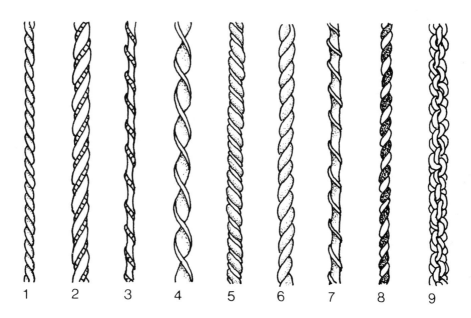

1   2   3   4   5   6   7   8   9

54 A selection of twists

bend the wire tightly and evenly round the rod. If you want to make a huge quantity of links or springs, secure a hand drill horizontally in the vice and fix the rod and wire in the drill chuck (**55**). Guide the wire with one hand, so that it is at right angles to the rod whilst you turn the drill handle with the other. Then release the rod from the vice or the chuck and burn away the paper by playing the gas flame on it. This will enable you to slide the wire off the rod. You now have a spring (**56**). To make the links, hold the spiral firmly in the first finger and thumb of one hand, rest them against the v-shaped notch in the pin and cut a straight line down the spiral. Keep the saw almost vertical to avoid cutting the other side of the spiral, thus making semi-circles instead of circles. If you want oval or square links, use an oval or square rod. The paper is important because its removal provides enough space between the spiral and rod to allow the spring to be slid off.

Having made the links, the next thing is to assemble them. Before closing the joins in the links, make sure that they are free from any burrs left by the saw.

It is wise to solder all the joins in a chain, but it is an extremely demanding process, especially if you are soldering a fine chain. The alternative to soldering is

97

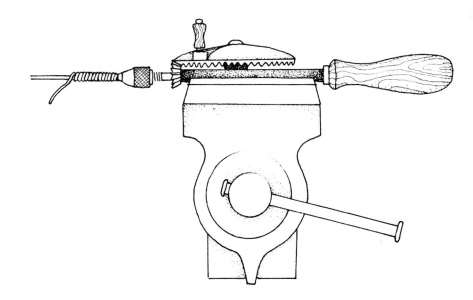

55 Making a spiral of round links

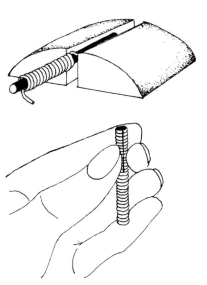

56 Cutting links

springing the joins together. Hold each link in two pairs of flat pliers or flat pliers and parallel pliers, as if you were closing a jump ring. First bend one side in line with the other side, then beyond it and back. Then bend the other one in the opposite direction and back, so that the two ends meet in a good join. This will put some spring or tension into the link, preventing it from bending open easily. Soldering a chain can be hazardous, because of the tendency of the solder to run from existing joins and to solder separate links together during heating. If you are making a long chain, solder half the links individually, then join them in pairs with a third link, then join the units of three to make units of seven and so on. If there are two sizes of link, solder the smaller ones first then link them with the larger ones.

To solder a link joining two others, or more, hold the link in the soldering tweezers, with the join uppermost, and direct the flame on the join, keeping it away from the other links. Alternatively, take a piece of hard metal wire, brass or steel for example, about 3in long. Bend a right-angle about $\frac{3}{4}$in from one end. Push the long side into the charcoal, and place the link to be soldered on the horizontal arm, join uppermost and heat it as described above.

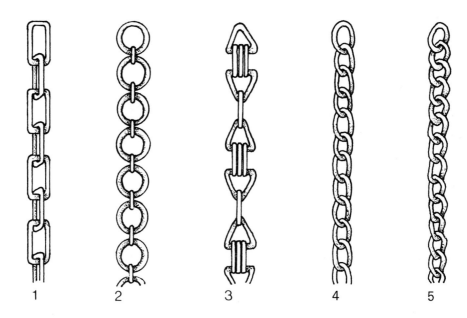

57 Five forms of chain

The ways of making chain are virtually endless. The links can be cut out or twisted; assembly patterns can be varied. Just a few are illustrated here, with indications for making them (**57, 58**).

1(**57**) Use a rectangular mandril and a thick gauge wire.

2 Use a large round mandril and thick gauge wire for the big round links and a small oval or rectangular mandril with thin gauge wire for the small links. Solder up the small links first and join them with the large links, using easy solder.

3 Use a triangular mandril and a narrow oblong one. Alternatively, take three long thin nails, cut off their heads and stick them into a block of soft wood so that they make a triangular former, round which you can wind the wire. Do the same for the oblong links, using two nails only. The size of the curve at either end of the oblong link will depend upon the thickness of the nails used. The disadvantage of this method is that you cannot make very long lengths of spirals. To join up the chain, solder the oblong links first, and connect them with the triangular ones.

58 Five more forms of chain

4 and 5 These are traditional chains. Use an oval mandril to make the links and join them up; 4 will not lie flat easily, but 5 will. To make 5, place 4 on the flattening stake with all the links lying the same way, and beat it with the wooden mallet. If the metal is too hard for this to have any effect, place another flat metal block over the chain and beat it with a hammer.

1 (**58**) For this chain, make two sets of oblong links. One set will be the short connecting links and the other, at least three times longer, will be the decorative ones. Solder up the longer ones. Put a thin nail or round mandril through each end and twist so that the central part forms a regular twist. Join them with the plain oblong links.

2 This is similar, but it needs three differently shaped links. The round and small oval links are made in the usual way on mandrils. The quickest way of making the figures-of-eight is by winding the wire in a figure-of-eight pattern round two nails stuck in soft wood, and then cutting through the resulting coil. The order in which you join this necklace is not particularly important.

3 This makes another use of the round coil or spiral. Turn up a length of round coil on a round mandril and cut off a length of ten circles with the snips. Hold one end of the coil in the parallel pliers, and bend the rest round to form a flower shape so that the ends are close to each other. To space the rings regularly, you will need to use a pair of flat pliers. If you use a thick gauge wire, the flower should be stable, but if it seems likely to pull open under any pressure, join the ends together and solder them. Make all the flowers first, then link them together with round links.

4 This has a unit of three rings linked together in the same way as Russian wedding rings are made. To make them, turn up a coil of round links which should be at least 10mm diameter. Anything smaller becomes difficult to handle and solder. Cut the links from the coil. Solder up one ring, put a second ring through the first and solder it up. Then link the third ring through both rings and solder that up. The effect is of one ring made up of three rings which overlap each other. To make the figure-of-eight links, a different method from that described for chain No. 2 above is advisable. Take a length of round wire and with the round pliers turn up a circle which will go round the three rings, holding them firmly. Allowing enough to make another circle, the same size, cut off the wire. Turn up the second circle in the opposite direction from the first so that you have a figure-of-eight. Attach a group of three rings to each side of this, opening the circles sideways, not uncurling them. Secure them with solder if necessary.

5 This is extremely simple but different from the previous chains, in that it incorporates a cut-out unit. The linked part is made up of oval links. The flat plates are cut from a strip of narrow sheet, the ends are filed round and drilled with a small hole through which the chain is passed. If the final piece is to be polished, it is advisable to polish the plate links before assembling them.

Filigree

Filigree is an old technique which is still used especially in the Mediterranean and the Middle East. Unfortunately, it is produced cheaply in huge quantities and fine examples are not often seen. It can, however, be very attractive and delicate if the design has fluid curves, the filigree wires are well spaced and it is well made. As the filigree wire is fine, it is soldered into a more robust frame. To make the illustrated pendant

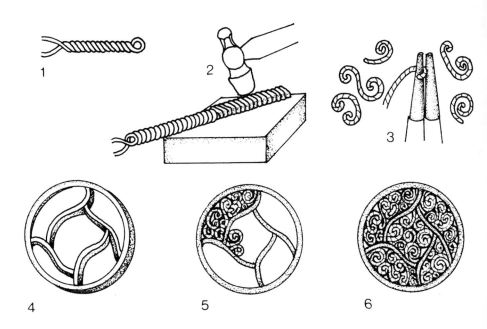

(**59, 6**), you need a length of flat wire at least
1·5 × 0·75mm for the frame. You can use thicker flat
wire or square wire according to your preference. For
the filigree wire you need round wire SWG 25, 5mm
thick.

First turn up the round frame with the thick wire and
solder it. Then arrange the four branches of the thick
wire and solder them together and to the circle (**59, 4**).
This arrangement provides a strong structure, into
which the filigree coils and twists can be soldered. To
make the filigree wire, make a double twist of the fine
wire and flatten it (**59, 1**). To do this use rolling mills if
they are available, otherwise place the wire on the
flattening stake and hammer it (**59, 2**) or place another
metal block over it and beat it with a heavy hammer.
This should flatten the twist uniformly. When it has
been annealed, it is ready to be used. With the round
nosed pliers, or the small half round pliers, bend the
filigree wire into short curls and curves (**59, 3**). Fit these
into the spaces formed by the thick wires, so that each
section is filled with pieces wedged into place (**59, 5**).
Then solder them carefully using tiny paillons of
solder. The best way to solder the piece is to raise it on a
wire platform so that you can get the flame underneath

it. Place the solder paillons on top of the joins and allow the heat from below to draw it downwards into the joins. It is important not to clog the filigree with solder, because you cannot remove it without damaging the filigree and it spoils the delicate look of the work. Solder on the loop and pickle the piece. To finish it, clean up the outside rim, removing any scratches. Then polish the outside rim and the loop and buff the top surface if you wish.

9 Fixtures and fittings

Safety catches for brooches, and screw ear fittings and the like are known as 'findings'. They are complicated and demanding to make. Therefore, it is often better to buy them, but mass produced butterfly ear-ring fittings tend to be somewhat flimsy and since they are simple to make, perhaps it is preferable to do so. Box catches for necklaces and bracelets are not easy to construct, but having once mastered them you can make a clasp which suits your design instead of having to compromise with whatever is available.

Hinges are useful in many different forms of jewellery, for example, to link the units in an articulated necklace or bracelet or for a brooch pin. To make a hinge, you need chenier or fine tubing, so before describing the process of making a hinge, I shall describe the method for making chenier. The equipment you will need in addition to the usual tools is as follows: a block of hard wood, the end grain surface of which is at least 2×3in, to be secured in the bench vice; a steel rod such as the shaft of a twist drill, diameter $\frac{1}{16}$in. A jeweller's hammer is adequate for the job, but a creasing or riveting hammer is the proper tool.

Cut a strip of BMG 8 sheet, 4in long and $\frac{3}{8}$in wide, which will produce a tube slightly under $\frac{1}{8}$in outside diameter. (The circumference is equal to three times the diameter of the circle, plus the thickness of the metal.) The sides of the strip must be straight and parallel. Taper $\frac{1}{2}$in at one end, leaving a blunt end, not a point (**60, 1**). In the end grain of the wood, cut and file a u-shaped groove slightly wider than $\frac{1}{8}$in. Place the strip over and exactly in line with the groove and lay the steel rod on top of it (**60, 2**). Tap along the rod with the hammer, until the strip is forced into the groove, forming a u-shape itself. If the wood groove is shorter than the strip, start forming the curve at one end of the strip and move the strip along the groove as you are forming it, so that the end of the rod does not make a ridge in the metal (**60, 3**). When the u-shaped curve is uniform along the whole length of the strip, tap the edges over the rod with the wedge shaped end of the jeweller's hammer, if you do not have a creasing hammer. The edges should meet, forming a rough tube, but they must not overlap (**60, 4**). If they do not meet all the way along, it does not matter at this stage. There is a tendency for the strip to twist, so that the join ceases to be a straight line. This happens when you have tapped part of one side too far over, it can be avoided with a systematic approach and regular, even hammering. Try to avoid distorting the edge when hammering.

Remove the steel rod and anneal the tube which will have been hardened by the hammering. The next step is to pull the tube through the draw plate. To retain the inside diameter of the tube when it is pulled, insert a length of straight greased steel piano wire. Insert the tapered end of the tube in a suitable hole in the round draw plate, lubricate with oil, and pull it and the wire through (**60, 5**). Repeat this until the join is properly closed. Saw off the tapered end. Before soldering the join, anneal and pickle the chenier, making sure no alum or acid is trapped inside it. Dry it and place small pieces of solder across the join. Heat it gently until the solder runs along the join. If you want to make a lot of tubing, it is worth investing in a swage block for forming the tube.

The method of making a hinge is always the same. Here it is described for the joint and clasp of the bracelet described in Chapter 6. Take some tubing at least as thick as the metal used for the bracelet. If you have to draw some tubing smaller, push into it a length of greased piano wire or steel rod to prevent the central aperture from being diminished at the same time. To remove the rod, saw off the tapered end, leaving the rod projecting beyond the tube. Pull out the piano wire by pulling it through a hole in the draw plate which is too small to allow the tube to pass through it. File a groove

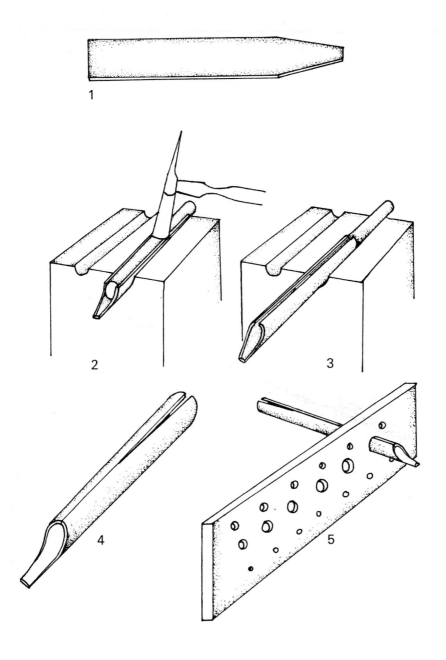

60 Making chenier
1 Strip cut and tapered
2 Strip hammered into grooved block
3 Moving the rod along the strip
4 Tubed strip
5 Tube drawn to close it up

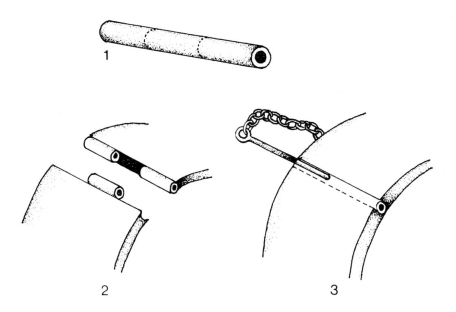

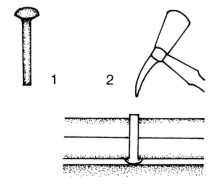

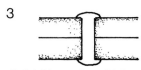

in both ends of both sides of the bangle with a round needle file. It is essential that these grooves are precise, because the alignment of the hinges depends upon it. Cut a length of tube slightly longer than the depth of the bracelet and cut it into three equal sections (**61, 1**). Solder the two outer sections into the groove on one side of the joint, and solder the central one on the other side, so that it fits exactly between the first two (**61, 2**). To make a pin to fit through the hinge, take a piece of wire which fits tightly into the tubing. Borax and heat one end until it melts into a ball. File the ball through half its diameter, so that it is flat topped (**62, 1**). Pass the wire through the hinge, and cut off the other end a fraction beyond the end of the tube. Place the flat head on a hard flat surface, and with the jeweller's hammer, spread the other end of the pin by tapping it (**62, 2**). This will hold the pin riveted in place (**62, 3**). To make the clasp, instead of riveting a pin through the hinge, take a length of the same gauge wire. Bend one end into a ring and secure it with solder, then cut off the other end, so that the pin is a little longer than the hinge. Attach the pin to the bracelet with a fine chain (**61, 3**).

To make a hinge for the second bangle described in Chapter 6, the basic method is the same, but because

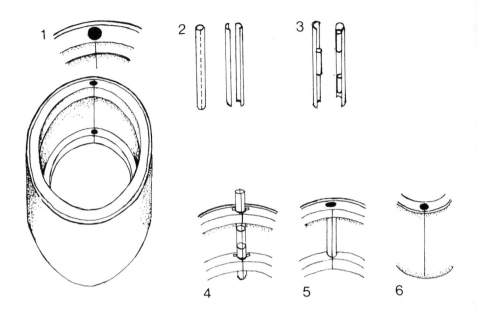

63 Making a hinge
1 Through the square wire frame drill a hole big enough to take the larger tube. Detail showing the position of the hole.
2 Cut the larger tube in half lengthways.
3 Solder the smaller hinge tubes inside the larger tube so that they fit together exactly.
4 Push the larger tube through the holes in the square wire frame, so that the tube joint will be in line with the cut to be made in the outside wall of the bracelet.
5 Saw and file the tube flush with the bracelet.
6 Cut through the outside wall of the bracelet.

the bangle is made of thin metal on a frame, there is nothing to solder the central tube of the hinge to. Instead, you have to make a round frame to hold the hinge (**63**). For this, you need a length of tube, a fraction narrower in diameter than the thickness of the outside edge of the bracelet, and another length of tube which will fit inside the first one. At the place where the hinge is to be, drill a hole through the frame wires and enlarge them with a round needle file so that the larger tube will fit through them (**63, 1**). Cut off a piece of the larger tube, a little longer than the width of the bracelet, and cut it in half length-wise, using a fine saw blade (**63, 2**). Prepare the three hinge units from the thinner tube and solder two inside one half of the large tube, and the central one inside the other half so that they will fit together exactly (**63, 3**). Then paint them with a little rouge to prevent the solder running during the next heating. Rouge prevents the solder running, but it is messy stuff and should be used sparingly. Fit the hinge's halves together and make sure that the outside surface is clean. Push it into the drilled holes and secure it in place with binding wire. The tube joints must lie across the edge of the bracelet, so that they will be in line with the ends of the bracelet when it is cut in half (**63, 4**). Use tiny paillons of easy solder on each side of the tube, using as little heat as possible. The chief danger is that the solder will run into the joint of the tube and spoil the entire piece. Having successfully soldered the tube in place, file it flush with the edge of the bracelet (**63, 5**). Leave the riveting until the clasp has been finished. If you use a hinge clasp, repeat the method just described. If you feel more ambitious, an invisible snap is described later in this chapter.

Brooch pin

Brooch pins and joints are easily made, as are simple catches; safety or roller catches on the other hand are best bought ready made. Nine carat gold makes better brooch pins than silver, because it is harder and does not bend. Before starting on the pin it is important to decide its position on the brooch. It must be no further than half-way down the brooch, otherwise the piece will become top heavy and fall forward. If the piece is delicate, make sure that the frame is strong enough to take the brooch pin; if it is not, reinforce it. Place the hinge on the right-hand side of the brooch back.

To make the pin and hinge, you need a length of wire for the pin and hinge rivet, and a small piece of BMG 8 or 10 for the joint. To make the joint, cut the shape illustrated (**64, 1**) in the appropriate size; with the parallel pliers, bend the joint round so that the two curved ends are parallel (**64, 2**). Drill through the curved ends, and solder the piece in position on to the brooch, supporting it if necessary with a cotter pin (**64, 3**). The solid side of the joint should be nearest the catch, because it provides a ridge over which the pin is sprung. At the same time, solder on the catch. If it is a simple wire catch, bend up a simple wire hook the right size, and hold it upright in place for soldering with a cotter pin. The opening of the hook should face the bottom of the brooch. If you are using a safety catch, it is very important to heat the area round the catch before heating the catch itself. The danger is that if the catch is heated first, it will draw up the solder, which will solder up the two component parts of the catch, rendering it useless.

To make the pin, melt one end of the wire into a bead, letting it drop to one side of the end of the wire (**64, 4**). Beat the bead flat on the flattening stake with a hammer, then file it into a circular shape which merges with the pin. Rest the pin on the joint and mark on the circle the point where the hinge pin should pass through it, then drill this mark (**64, 5**). If you are using silver for the brooch pin, it will need to be hardened at this stage. To do this, hold the hinge end in parallel pliers,

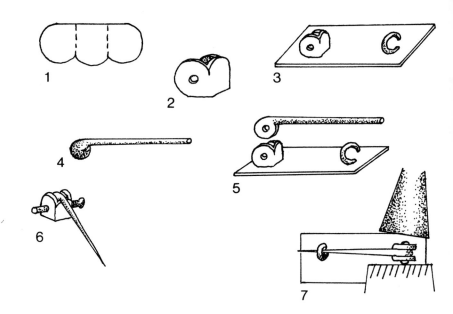

64 Preparing brooch catch
1 The joint
2 Joint bent into shape
3 Joint and catch in position for soldering
4 End of pin melted into a bead
5 Pin drilled in line with joint and filed to a point
6 Pin and joint assembled for riveting
7 Pin riveted to joint

the other end in a pin vice, or pliers, and twist the wire four or five times holding it as taut as possible so that it does not kink. Cut off the brooch pin to the right length, file up a point on the end, and polish it. The pin must then be riveted into the hinge by the method used for the bracelet hinge above (**64, 6 and 7**). The ridge of the joint should keep the pin so taut that it will not slip out of a simple catch.

Clasps

There are several types of clasp for bracelets and necklaces, one of which has already been described in the section on hinges in this chapter.

Simple hook clasps can be used for necklaces, because the weight of the necklace prevents the hook from slipping out of its ring. For a hook clasp you need a length of wire, the gauge of which should be suited to the proportions of the necklace. A light, delicate necklace can be secured with fine wire, whilst a heavy one needs a thicker wire. With the half round nosed pliers, make a long hook, the shape of a shepherd's crook, with a narrow opening (**65, 1**). Bend the short

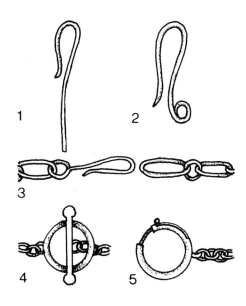

end out slightly so that it will slip easily into a ring. Bend up a small ring on the long end of the hook, in order to attach it to the necklace (**65, 2**). If you wish to secure a silver hook to the necklace with solder, do this before bending up the hook. First turn up the link ring in the end of the wire, connect it to the necklace and solder it up. Then hold the wire taut and twist it four or five times to harden it as described for the brooch pin. Finally bend it up into a hook. Then prepare a ring to take the hook and solder it up at the other end of the chain (**65, 3**).

A ring and bar clasp is more secure than a hook, and can safely be used for bracelets as well as necklaces. Select the wire thickness and size of the clasp in the same way as for a hook fastening. Cut off a piece of wire twice as long as the final length you require. Borax and melt both ends into round beads. Turn up four small jump rings and solder one to the centre of the crossbar. Turn up and solder a ring smaller in diameter than the length of the crossbar, then solder to it a jump ring the same size as the one on the cross bar. Link each piece to the rest of the necklace or bracelet with a jump ring (**65, 4**). Both these clasps are suitable to be used with the chains described in Chapter 8.

Bolt rings are the round safety clasps with a spring fastener, which are widely available commercially (**65, 5**). The spring mechanism is operated by a coil, usually made of copper which will loose its spring if it is heated and annealed. To avoid this, bolt rings must be attached with soft or lead solder, which require little heat and not gold or silver solder.

A box catch is more secure than any of the clasps mentioned above, but it is also much more difficult to make, and its success depends upon very precise work. The catch described is rectangular, but the same principle can also be used for square, round or tubular ones.

First cut two perfect rectangles from BMG 8, one $\frac{1}{2} \times \frac{3}{8}$in, the other $\frac{1}{8} \times \frac{3}{8}$in and file the edges true. Solder the smaller rectangle across and at right angles to one of the shorter sides of the larger rectangle, holding it in place with cotter pins to do so (**66, 1**). If this proves too difficult, make the base plate longer, and solder the cross piece a little distance from the end. Then cut off the excess base plate flush with the cross piece. On the cross piece mark a line parallel with the upper and lower edges just under $\frac{1}{16}$in from the solder joint, and $\frac{1}{16}$in from either end. At the centre of the line, mark a notch $\frac{1}{16}$in long and $\frac{1}{32}$in above the line. Drill and saw this area out down to the base plate (**66, 2**). Solder a strip of flat or square wire $\frac{1}{16}$in wide on both sides of the base plate, flush with the edges (**66, 2**). Next make the tongue for the clasp. To do this, cut a strip $\frac{1}{4} \times 1\frac{1}{8}$in from a sheet of hardened BMG 6 (**66, 3**). From one end cut out two rectangles $\frac{3}{32} \times \frac{1}{8}$in leaving a central projecting piece $\frac{1}{8}$ long by $\frac{1}{16}$in wide which will form the thumb piece of the clasp. Cut out and solder a rectangle $\frac{1}{8} \times \frac{1}{16}$in to the thumb piece. To the other end on the same side of the metal, solder a jump ring which will link the tongue to the necklace or bracelet. Then beat it with a mallet to reharden the metal. Just under $\frac{1}{2}$in from the jump ring end and on the opposite side of the metal from the jump ring and thumb piece, score a deep line across the strip and, using parallel pliers, bend the metal over at that line until the upper and lower parts are almost parallel (**65, 4**). The tongue should go through the aperture in the crosspiece and spring up so that either side of the thumb piece is held behind the cross piece. Check that the tongue is not longer than the base plate, and file off any excess if necessary. Cut a rectangle of BMG 8 $\frac{3}{8} \times \frac{5}{32}$in, and solder it to the end of the base plate, parallel with the cross piece. Then cut another rectangle $\frac{3}{8} \times \frac{17}{32}$in (ie just over $\frac{1}{2}$in) and solder it with easy solder to the two cross pieces, forming a roof for the clasp. In order to join it to the piece of jewellery it has been made for, solder a jump ring to the end wall of the clasp (**66, 6**).

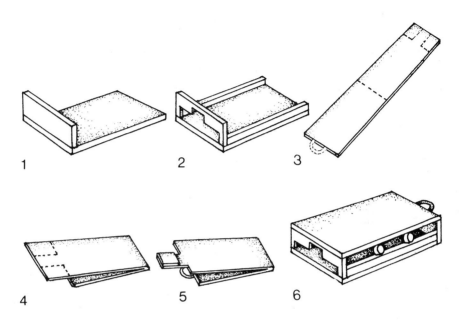

66 A box clasp
1 Base plate and cross piece
2 Cross piece cut out ready to hold clasp; wire soldered down edges
3 Strip for clasp tongue
4 Folded tongue before cutting out
5 Folded tongue with thumb piece
6 Completed box clasp

A variation on the box catch just described, is the catch built into a necklace or bracelet so that it is invisible. To start with, a word of warning: this fitting is perhaps even more exacting and hazardous than the ordinary box catch, again requiring very precise work. When you can make one of these well, you have become a highly skilled craftsman.

The catch is described here for use in a bangle, but the same principle can be used for necklaces and bracelets of overlapping links, or solid collars which are hinged in the front. The bangle in this case is built on a wire frame and is the second one described in Chapter 6. The clasp is the last part to be made, after any decoration has been applied and the hinge described earlier in this chapter has been soldered in. The bangle is still in one piece at this stage, so to cut it in two (63, 6), file a fine groove down the outside surface, level with the centre of the hinge, and a second groove opposite the hinge where the clasp is to be. Saw down these lines and join the hinge temporarily with a piece of wire passed through it.

To make the snap, first cut two rectangles from BMG 8 which will fit across the join of the bracelet, the same depth and width as the bracelet, for the face

(**67, 3**) and for the backplate (**67, 1**) of the clasp. In this clasp, the tongue is made in two sections, which are soldered to each other, instead of one section which is bent over on itself. Next, cut two strips from BMG 6 to form the bottom plate and spring plate of the snap (**67, 1**). The bottom plate should be the same width as the gap between the frame wires (**67, 1a**), and about $\frac{5}{16}$in long; the spring plate should be half that width and shorter than the base plate by the thickness of BMG 8 (**67, 1d**).

Solder the base plate at right angles to the backplate (**67, 2**). Next solder the spring plate on to the end of the baseplate, so that the end nearest the backplate is separated from the baseplate by a space at least the thickness of the metal (**67, 2**). To do this, separate the baseplate and spring plate with a piece of metal such as an old, thick saw blade or a piece of thick brass or ferrous wire, whilst soldering. It is also important to support the backplate during heating. Now cut an aperture in the face plate for the tongue, so that the two snap plates fit through it, and solder it in place over the edge of the bangle join with the spring plate notch nearest the outside of the bangle (**67, 3**). From the centre of the spring plate notch, saw a line up to the bangle outside surface and through the surface for $\frac{1}{16}$in using a thick saw blade (**67, 4**). The thumb piece will project through this space (**67, 6**).

Next cut two identical pieces of BMG 8 which will form the roof or lining of the catch. They should be as wide as the bangle and $\frac{3}{8}$in long. Solder both these pieces in, at both ends of the join parallel with the bracelet wall, so that each projects beyond the end of the bracelet by the thickness of BMG 8. This projection is to accommodate the face plate and the backplate of the catch.

Soldering the snap in place is the most hazardous part of this construction (**67, 5**). It has to be done with the bangle closed (**67, 6**), so there is considerable danger of previous solder joins melting or running into the wrong place. To avoid this, carefully paint both sides of the clasp with rouge. Keep the back of the backplate and the end to which it is to be joined, clean, scraping them if necessary. Assemble the clasp and keep the bracelet shut by binding it together with binding wire. Place very small pieces of solder along the join between the backplate and the end of the bracelet and heat the area of the join carefully, until the solder runs. Open the bangle by inserting a knife through the thumb piece notch and pressing on the spring. Remove the rouge with a toothbrush and hot soapy water; then pickle the piece and file off any excess solder. Finally make a thumb piece

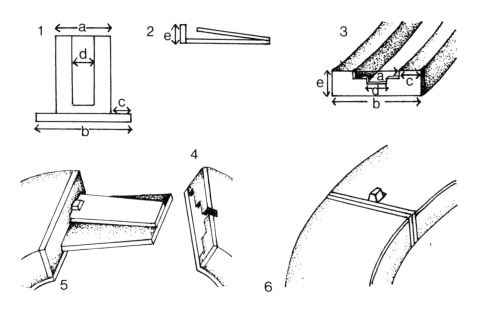

67 A box clasp inside a bracelet
1 Top view of the backplate of the clasp, soldered to the bottom plate and spring plate which form the clasp tongue
2 Side view of the backplate, bottom plate and spring plate
3 The face plate soldered to the bracelet
4 The face plate soldered to the bracelet, completed with a lining or roof
5 The clasp tongue showing lining
6 Clasp, closed showing the thumb piece

which will fit through the notch and project about $\frac{1}{32}$in above the surface of the bangle. Solder it on to the spring plate, supporting the plate as you do so. The clasp is now complete, and it only remains to rivet the hinge permanently.

Ear clips

There are several different types of ear clip fitting, the main difference between them being that between fittings for pierced ears and for unpierced ears. The latter are either secured with a screw or a clip, whilst those for pierced ears are secured by a hook or a peg and butterfly or scroll. Screw ear fittings are best purchased ready made as are clip fittings.

The simplest fitting for pierced ears is a plain hook. Take two pieces of wire $1\frac{1}{2}$in to 2in long, of any gauge between 18 and 24 SWG. Taper one end of each to a blunt point, using a needle file. With the half round pliers, bend a hook $\frac{1}{2}$in to $\frac{3}{4}$in from the pointed end of each. Bend the short end inwards, then outwards at the end, and bend the long side inwards at the opening (see 34, 4). Hooks are most suitable for drop ear-rings, so at the long end of the hook, bend up a ring with round nosed pliers, which can be connected with the ear-ring

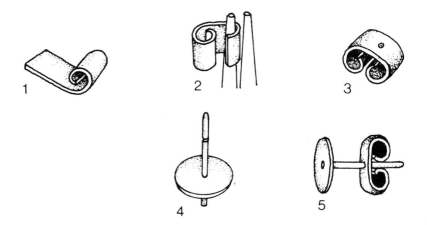

68 Ear-ring fittings
1–3 Turning up end of butterfly scroll
4 Pin and cup
5 Assembled pin and scroll

piece. Alternatively, spread the long end by beating it with a hammer on the flattening stake, and solder it to the back of the ear-ring piece.

For stud ear-rings peg and scroll fittings are preferable. To make these, you need a length of wire between SWG 18 and 24, and a strip of BMG 8. Straighten the wire, and cut off two lengths just over $\frac{1}{2}$in long. Taper one end of each to a blunt point and file a shallow groove round the peg, $\frac{1}{8}$in from the point. Cut two strips of the sheet $\frac{5}{8} \times \frac{3}{16}$in. Mark the centre and with round nosed pliers, turn in the ends to form two scrolls which touch each other. Then drill a hole in the centre, the same diameter as the peg (**68, 1–3**). The peg should be able to pass through the hole and be held by the scrolls. Adjust the scrolls if the peg is either loose or held so tightly that it is difficult to push through. To make a plain metal stud ear-ring, either solder a bead to the end of the peg, or cut out a flat circle and drill the centre with a hole the same diameter as the peg, so that the peg can be soldered into it (**68, 4**). Do not solder the peg with the scroll on it, because the scroll will be annealed and loose its spring. For pearl studs, using half drilled pearls, make two small domed cups, drill them through the centre, pass the peg through the hole, so that it projects enough to hold the pearl. Solder the peg in place then glue the pearl to the peg and to the cup with pearl cement. The illustration shows a plain round disc, to which a decorative ear-ring can be soldered (**68, 5**). Fix the peg to a stud ear-ring anywhere between the centre and the top of the ear-ring, but not below the centre, because it will fall forward in the ear. When making stud ear-rings, it is important to bear in mind that the ear lobe is very soft and unable to support much weight; if the ear-rings weigh more than $\frac{1}{4}$oz, they will fall forwards.

Cuff links

There are two ways to hold cuff links together; with links, or with rigid or sprung backs. The traditional way to link cuff links is with five oval links and two jump rings which are soldered to both sides of the cuff links. The distance between the two links should be $\frac{11}{16}$in, which makes each link just under $\frac{3}{16}$in long. Solder up two links and connect them with a third. These will be the central three links. Turn up two round jump rings and solder one in the centre of the back of each cuff link (**69, 1**). With a fourth link, connect the three links and the jump ring on one side (**69, 2**). Solder the link in the same way as you would for a chain, either holding it in tweezers or balancing it on a wire hook to isolate it as far as possible from the rest of the piece and from previous solder joins (**69, 3, 4**). Repeat this process in order to join on the other side of the link.

There are several variations on this method. Three links instead of five gives a slightly more rigid link, whilst one long narrow link is quicker to make and just as effective. The alternative to links, a spring or rigid back, is obtainable commercially. These are for cuff links of which one side only is decorative and the other side is provided by the fitting itself (which is not very attractive). To make a rigid fitting which accommodates both sides of the cuff links is not difficult. Cut a curved arm from a reasonably thick gauge of metal, at least BMG 12, to ensure that it does not bend in use and provides an adequate soldering base. Pierce out one end, and solder the other to the front unit of the cuff link (**70, 1, 2**). If you want the front unit to lie in any particular direction, line it up accordingly with the arm. From BMG 12 or thicker, cut a bridge or link which will be soldered to the back unit (**70, 3**). The pierced area of the arm must be able to swivel in the bridge. Pass the bridge through the pierced portion of the arm, and solder it to the back unit (**70, 4**). If this

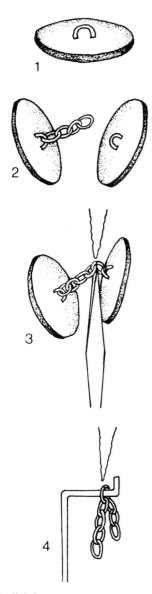

69 Cuff link
1 Back with soldered jump ring
2 Soldering links
3, 4 Joint halves of cuff link

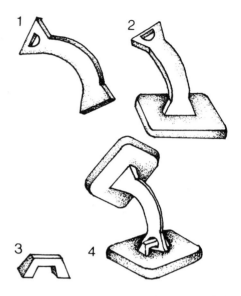

70 Rigid arm cuff link
1 Curved arm
2 Arm soldered to front
3 The bridge
4 Bridge, arm and back assembled

proves too difficult to balance, solder one side of the bridge to the back unit and bend up the other side far enough to allow the pierced part of the arm to be linked on to it. Then, press it down again and solder it.

When buying spring cuff link backs, it is advisable to ask how they should be attached, because there are a number of types, each requiring different treatment.

10 Decorative processes

A variety of decorative processes are now described. The first three: texturing, colouring, and etching the metal, are relatively simple methods of finishing the surface of a piece, whilst granulation, engraving, inlay and niello work are more ambitious techniques.

Texturing is normally the final stage, and replaces polishing. In fact the simplest way to give a piece a matt finish is with emery paper. The degree of texturing depends upon the grade of paper used, and for the cleanest looking result, always rub the emery paper in the same direction. To achieve a slightly deeper texture, use a brass brush, either a hand brush or a brass wire wheel on the polishing machine. Small brass end brushes are also available to use on the pendant drill and are particularly useful for reaching areas which you cannot polish. A glass brush gives a finer satin finish, again the best effect is achieved by making all the strokes in the same direction.

The glass brush is made of fine strands of glass bound together with string, and as you use it, tiny flakes of glass break off, so be very careful not to inhale these splinters or get them in your hands; collect them in a piece of paper which you can throw away immediately.

Many different textures can be arrived at by beating the metal, either with a hammer or with punches. There is a danger of stretching the metal by beating it, so if you want a beaten texture on an exactly made piece, for example on an exactly round pendant, you will probably have to file the piece true again, after it has been beaten. It is however, suitable for less precisely finished work. Use the round end of the ballpein hammer, or either end of the jeweller's hammer. Support the piece (for example, a ring can be supported on the triblet), and beat the metal with regular strokes.

To make a texturing punch, take a steel rod and cut a design into one end. You can saw straight lines across it one way, or at right angles to each other to form a check or use different sized sawblades, or cut and file more complicated designs. When using the punch, beat it with a regular stroke, to achieve a regular depth and effect. You can improvise with different things, such as round headed nails, using the round head as a punch, or steel washers, or brass mesh which you lay on the surface to be textured and hammer it down. There is enormous scope for inventing different textures.

Colouring the metal

Silver tarnishes naturally if it is exposed to the atmosphere, because the sulphur in the air reacts with the silver. This process can be achieved quickly, by oxidizing the surface with sulphur. Various compounds of sulphur produce different colours. The depth of colour depends upon the length of time the silver is exposed to the solution and upon the strength of it. Ammonium sulphide is the most usual sulphide used, it gives a range of colour to the polished silver surface, from pale golden straw, through deep crimson to blue-black. Potassium sulphide or barium sulphide can also be used. A mixture of three parts hydrochloric acid, one part iodine and one part water will produce green when applied to silver.

Before applying any of these solutions, the piece must be clean. Mix up and heat the required solution. To acquire an overall effect, immerse the piece in the solution. Alternatively, paint it on with a paint brush watching carefully for the colours you require. When this moment is reached, quickly wash the piece in water and dry it. You can then buff it, or rub it with chamois to highlight some areas. If you find that the colour comes off very easily, it means that the solution was too strong, and if spots appear it means that the piece was not properly cleaned to start with. Alloyed gold can be coloured in the same way as silver, but it has to be heated until it is too hot to hold. If a piece is set with soft stones, such as turquoise or lapis, do not immerse it in any of the solutions, also avoid darkening the metal behind open settings, because the fire and colour of the stone will be dulled.

The chemicals are obtainable from large chemists. They should be stored in enamelled or earthenware jars, and used in a well ventilated room.

Etching

Etching a pattern on metal is done by painting parts of the surface with acid resistant varnish (etching ground) and then placing the piece in acid. The unpainted areas are eaten in by the acid, leaving the varnished parts in relief. The longer the metal remains in the acid, the deeper the etched parts will be. For this process you need thick gauge copper or silver BMG 16/18; gold can also be etched but it is of course costly. The other necessary equipment is etching ground, two camel hair brushes, a fine one and a thick one, eg Nos 2 and 5, two rubber or glass developing trays, a glass container for mixing the acid, nitric acid, turpentine, soft string, blotting paper and emery paper Grade 0.

Draw the design out first on paper. The varnish is applied with paint brushes, so designs with flowing lines and curves are more suitable than precise patterns with sharp corners and a lot of detail.

To prepare the metal, rub it with emery paper to remove all dirt and grease. This is essential, because the etching ground will not adhere to the metal if it is not clean. To test that it is clean, dip the metal in water. If it is clean, a film of water will cling to the entire surface of the metal.

Without touching the metal surface with your fingers, transfer the design to the metal with carbon paper. To avoid confusing the areas to be blocked out with those to be etched, paint on the drawing the parts to be varnished. With the fine camel hair brush, paint out those parts on the metal. Apply the varnish evenly, making the brush strokes in the same direction as far as possible. Leave it to dry for three or four hours. When it is dry, paint out the other side and the edges using the thick brush. Then leave it to dry again.

The next stage is to prepare the acid. CAUTION: DO NOT INHALE THE ACID FUMES, OR SPILL IT ON YOURSELF OR YOUR CLOTHES. If you do splash acid on your hands, wash them immediately with soap and plenty of running water. If it gets on your clothes, rinse them with plenty of water and some household ammonia.

Place both developing trays on a table, and half fill one with water. The other one is for the nitric acid. Mix the acid in a glass container in the proportions of two parts water to one part acid. First pour the water into the glass then add the acid slowly. NEVER ADD WATER TO ACID. One part acid to two parts water is the strongest solution advisable. One part acid to three parts water will make the etching process slower, but the lines will be sharper. A strong acid solution will sometimes lift the edges of the varnish, but a weaker solution does not. Pour the solution into the empty tray. The reaction of the water and acid generates heat, so leave the solution to cool for 15 to 20 minutes. If used warm, the action of the acid on the metal generates more heat which can soften the varnish and cause it to lift.

Use the string to lift the metal in and out of the acid. If the piece is a flat sheet of metal, place two lengths of string under it; if it is a ring, thread the string through it. Put the piece in the acid and after two or three minutes, check the speed of the etch. If the etching process is working properly, the unvarnished areas will be covered with tiny gas bubbles. These bubbles will leave a pitted effect on the metal. If you prefer a smoother finish, you have to break the bubbles, by frequently lifting the piece out of the acid. Each time you remove the piece from the acid, rinse it in the water, and examine the varnish for cracks or pinhole breaks. If there is a crack, dry the piece on blotting paper and leave it to dry out completely in the air for 15 to 20 minutes. Then patch up the cracks and again leave it until the fresh varnish is completely dry. When the etched parts are as deep as you want them to be, rinse and dry the piece. Then remove the etching ground with turpentine, and polish the piece lightly. Heavy polishing will smooth the sharp etched lines and reduce the contrast between the etched and unetched parts.

Granulation

Granulation is the method of decorating a smooth surface with hundreds of tiny granules without using any solder. The technique was perfected between 800 and 300 BC by the Etruscans, but the secret was then lost until the 1930s. Attempts to make granulation with solder are marred by the clogged effect the solder gives.

First make the granules in uniform sizes by cutting pieces from gold or silver wire using the snips. Drop these on to a layer of crushed charcoal, making sure that they are all separated from each other, then cover them with another thin layer of crushed charcoal. Heat the charcoal red hot so that the pieces of wire melt, forming tiny beads. Cool the charcoal slowly, then empty it into a bowl of water and detergent. The charcoal will float off whilst the granules will remain at the bottom of the bowl. They should not need to be pickled because the surrounding charcoal should have prevented oxidation. Clean the metal which the granulation is to decorate, by heating it and quenching it in half-and-half solution of water and nitric acid. Then rinse it well. The granules are attached to the metal initially with a thin paste of organic glue. Use gum tragacanth or fish glue and mix it in equal quantity with a copper salt such as powdered cupric hydroxide [$Cu(OH)_2$], add water to make a paste, pick up each granule on a fine paint brush and place it in position on the metal surface. Decide upon the pattern or decoration you want to make with the beads before applying them. When they are all in place, heat the piece very slowly with an orange, reduced flame. The low flame creates an envelope almost without oxygen, which prevents a high rate of oxidation on the metal. Continue to heat the piece until the surface melts slightly, at which point the actual joining of the granules occurs and the flame must be removed immediately. (When heat is applied, the glue carbonizes and the cupric hydroxide becomes cupric oxide. The oxygen in the oxide then combines with the carbon and the carbon reduces the copper oxide to copper whilst the rest is dissipated as carbon dioxide gas. A film of copper forms and joins the grain to the metal base at the point of contact only.) Cupric hydroxide must be used with pure gold or silver, but the copper in an alloyed or lower carat gold may form the join without the addition of a copper salt. However it is wise to use some cupric hydroxide in the organic glue to ensure the join. Judging the moment at which the copper has run and formed the join is difficult; of course the danger is that you may overheat and melt the whole article. Experience is the only way to learn when to remove the heat. There is a wide margin between the melting point of gold 1945·4°F/1063°C, and the point at which the joining occurs at 1643°F/890°C, but alloyed golds have lower melting points, and silver melts at 1640°F/893°C which leaves very little margin for error. All the granules should be attached in one firing, and the piece must be cooled gradually.

Flattened beads, pieces of wire and rectangular sections can also be used in the design, and attached in the same way. When applying the granules to a three-dimensional piece, allow the glue to dry on one surface

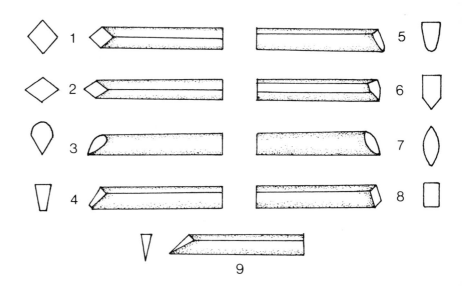

before applying any more to the next surface. Initially it is wise to confine yourself to two dimensional designs and master the technique before embarking on three-dimensional work.

Engraving

Engraving is a skill which requires much practice to master. The difficulty is to achieve control over the tool, so that you can engrave whatever line you want, strong continuous lines, short lines, straight or curved lines, co-ordinating your hand and your eyes. However, the technique is not complicated, and simple but effective results can be achieved by a beginner.

The tools, which are like chisels, are known as gravers, burins or scorpers. They are tempered steel rods, in a variety of shapes, held in a wooden handle. The gravers and the handles are sold separately. There are nine sections or shapes of graver generally available. Each one is obtainable in about six different sizes (**71**).

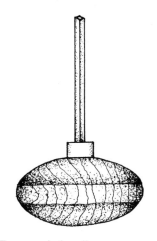

72 Engraver in handle

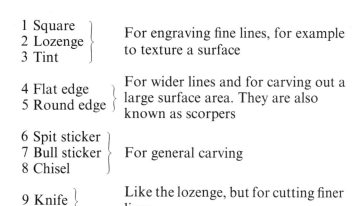

1 Square	}	For engraving fine lines, for example to texture a surface
2 Lozenge		
3 Tint		
4 Flat edge	}	For wider lines and for carving out a large surface area. They are also known as scorpers
5 Round edge		
6 Spit sticker	}	For general carving
7 Bull sticker		
8 Chisel		
9 Knife	}	Like the lozenge, but for cutting finer lines

The handles are ball shaped, pear shaped or mushroom shaped, to suit individual preferences, and are made to fit into the palm of the hand. Personally I find the mushroom shaped handles the most comfortable to use (72). The gravers are sold deliberately too long, so that you can shorten them to suit the size of your hand. To do this, secure the graver vertically in the vice with the excess length projecting above it, and strike with a hammer, so that the excess breaks off cleanly. To fix on the handle, raise the graver in the vice so that about 1in projects above it, then hammer the handle on with a mallet.

Hold the graver with the handle in the palm of the hand, towards the ball of the little finger, lay the thumb along the left hand edge of the graver (if you are right handed), and the first two fingers pressing against the other side (73, 1). The point of the graver should not project more than $\frac{1}{2}$in to $\frac{3}{4}$in beyond the end of the thumb. The thumb acts as a guide and a brake, whilst the graver is driven by the pressure of the palm. The lower side of the thumb should rest on the metal, so that as you push the graver, its side runs along the thumb pad. For your first engraved design, short straight lines are the wisest choice, because they are the easiest to perfect. The metal must be held firmly whilst you are engraving on it. Small pieces of metal, up to about $1\frac{1}{2}$in square are best secured in setting cement or sealing wax on the end of a piece of dowel. For larger pieces a round leather sandbag is the best support (73, 2). The design should be marked on the flat metal with a scriber, before you begin to engrave it. To start the engraving, hold the graver at about 45° to the metal, and drive it into the metal at the beginning of a scribed line; when the point has penetrated the metal surface, reduce the angle between the graver and the metal and cut along the centre of the line, driving the point upwards at the end. In other words, when you start the line, your elbow will be six or nine inches above the level of your hand, and will lower to almost the same

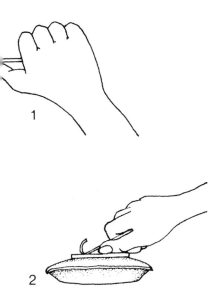

1

2

73 Engraving
1 Holding the graver
2 Position of the hand for engraving, with the metal supported on a leather sandbag

level when you are cutting the line. In time you will find the cutting angle which suits you best. If the graver makes an increasingly deep line and gets stuck, the angle at which you are holding it is too steep and may cause the point to break off. If on the other hand the graver slips out of the line you are engraving, it is being held too close to parallel with the metal. To make a long straight line, cut the first part as long as you can comfortably manage without moving your thumb, then keep the graver in the line and move your hand along to cut the next part. If you remove the graver in the middle, it will probably leave a burr and the width of the line will vary at the point where you have stopped and started again. As the graver cuts, a tiny coil of metal should rise like a thread in front of the point of the graver. If this coil emerges from either side of the line it is because the graver is not dead central.

To make a curve or a circle, start the line then move the metal round, not your hand which is holding the graver. If you are using a sandbag, the pressure exerted by the graver and the hand holding it in place, should be enough to hold the metal in place, whilst you move the sandbag round. If you do have to hold the metal down with your free hand, make sure that that hand is not in front of the graver. If the graver slips suddenly you can cut yourself badly.

It is essential to keep the gravers sharp whilst using them. Sharpening a graver properly is akin to polishing. First grind it on an India stone, lubricated with oil. Hold the cutting edge onto the stone, check that it is at the correct angle and carefully rub it up and down holding it at the same angle all the time. Check frequently that the angle is correct, and that you are not removing the sides of the cutting edge, by letting the graver swing from side to side. Deciding upon the angle at which to sharpen the graver is also a matter of personal preference which depends on how steep an angle you hold your arm when you engrave. Initially sharpen the graver so that the angle which you grind off is at 45° to the shaft of the graver and as you develop your own style you can decide for yourself whether this angle is right for you or not. It is easier to resharpen an already well sharpened graver than to correct one which has been rounded. When you are satisfied that the cutting edge is true, repeat the process on an Arkansus stone, which is finer than India stone. Finish the process by rubbing the graver edge on fine emery so that it is highly polished. A well sharpened tool is easier to use than a blunt one and will leave a clean line with no burr along its edges. To protect the gravers when they are not in use, stick them in a large piece of cork or hang them in a rack.

74 Designs for engraving

To engrave the inside of a concave shape, the cutting angle has to be changed. A graver ground in the usual way so that it appears as if the shaft of the graver has been sliced diagonally is impossible to use for this purpose. Instead it has to be sharpened so that in section it appears that the graver has been sliced diagonally in two opposing directions. This means grinding off the metal underneath the point of the graver so that the point occurs one third to one half through the thickness of the graver. The top surface must then be ground to form an angle of 45° with the new base of the cutting edge. Ground like this, the graver can be held at the correct angle to engrave the inside of a bowl or cup shape.

Initially straight lines can be used in many different ways to make patterns (74). Try starting with a series of parallel straight lines, very close to each other gradually becoming wider spaced. This gives a tonal effect which can be developed further, for example by using gravers of different widths. Another way of using straight lines is to engrave them radiating from a centre, again using different graver sizes, or arranging the lines in a repeating rhythm near and far from each other. This could be done on a large scale, covering a whole surface, either using dotted lines or continuous long lines, alternatively you could repeat the idea on a small scale to form a pattern of little flower like motifs. Cross-hatching produces some interesting effects, with the lines at right angles to each other, or crossing each other diagonally. Short gentle curves are the easiest to engrave to start with and again you can build up interesting patterns with the rhythmic use of small repeated curves. Representational or figurative designs are the most difficult to achieve, but they too become easier with practice. Learning to engrave is very much like learning to write or to draw. Once you have mastered it, you can produce any effect you want on metal. In fact if you can already draw, engraving will probably come easily to you.

An engraved design can be used as the chief decorative feature of a piece of jewellery, for example on an otherwise plain metal pendant or on the flat top of a ring like a signet ring, or on the links of a bracelet. If you make a bracelet of engraved linked units, first make up the individual units and finish them to the point when they are ready to be hinged together, then engrave each link separately and finally assemble the whole piece. Engraving can also be used as an attractive adjunct to stone set work, or pieces built up three dimensionally with several layers of metal. Try decorating the setting and shoulders of a solid stone set

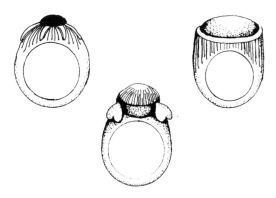

Engraved designs on a ring

ring with engraved lines or solder thin strips of metal round the setting, radiating out from it and engrave tendril like lines between the strips (**75**). Engraved links incorporated in a chain is another idea to play with.

Niello and inlay work

Niello and inlay both involve engraving. Niello is a black alloy of silver, copper, lead and sulphur which is used to fill the recesses of an engraved pattern so that the gold or silver design left proud is contrasted with a black background. A similar effect is achieved by applying a raised pattern of metal wire, or pierced metal sheet to a smooth metal background, providing a network of cells which are filled with the molten niello alloy. These two techniques are also used as the foundation for enamel work and are known as champlevé and cloisonné.

The technique is an old one and many old recipes exist for niello. The ingredients are always the same but the proportions used in different countries and different epochs varied. The following recipe is reliable:

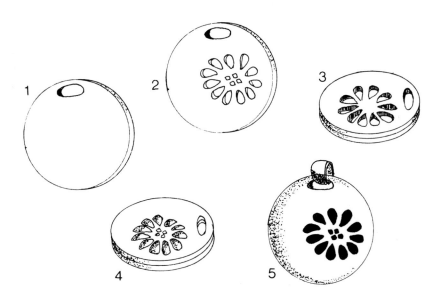

76 Niello
1 Base plate
2 Top plate with pierced design
3 Base plate and top plate soldered together
4 Powdered niello placed in pierced design
5 Finished piece

Fine silver – 6 parts
Fine copper – 2 parts
Fine lead – 1 part
Flowers of sulphur – 10 parts

All the metal ingredients must be unalloyed.

As for quantities, you will not require very much niello initially. Pennyweights, written dwt, are the traditional sub-division of troy ounces used for weighing precious metal, so if you acquire a set of pennyweights, interpret each part as representing 1 dwt. Alternatively, interpret each part as representing $\frac{1}{16}$oz. The above quantities will provide almost an ounce of niello. Melt the silver and copper with some borax in a crucible. When they are melted and fused add the lead well mixed with sulphur in a twist of paper. Mix them together thoroughly with a dry stick, then pour the liquid quickly into another small crucible in which the sulphur has already been placed. Remelt the niello and pour it out on to an iron or steel slab. Then beat it thin with a hammer whilst it is still hot. If it cools before you have beaten it thin, warm it with the blowpipe and beat it until it is about $\frac{1}{16}$in thick. It is now ready for use.

HEAT THE MIXTURE IN A WELL VENTILATED ROOM, BECAUSE IT CONTAINS LEAD, WHICH GIVES OFF POISONOUS FUMES.

The piece to be decorated should be made of sheet no thinner than BMG 14, which will allow you to cut out clearly the parts which are to be black. As with engraving, make your first niello design on flat metal. The complexity of the design depends upon your confidence and dexterity in engraving. Thin lines must be $\frac{1}{32}$ in deep so that they hold enough niello for it to be strong black; if the line is too shallow, the niello will be so thin as to appear grey. Large areas must be cut away evenly with the scorper, so that no part shows through the niello when the piece is being finished. Leave a metal border round the edge of the piece, so that the niello will not be vulnerable to chipping.

A pierced design for the niello provides an ideal alternative to champlevé, if you do not feel confident engraving (**76**). Cut two identical circles in BMG 14 and pierce both to take a hanging loop (**76, 1**). Scribe a simple design on one of the circles and with a piercing saw, cut it out (**76, 2**). Using hand solder, attach the pierced circle to the backing plate, taking care not to clog the holes with solder (**76, 3**).

When the piece is ready, grind up a piece of the prepared niello, until it is like fine sand. This is best done with a pestle and mortar, but a smooth hard stone such as a piece of agate and a slab of stone such as marble will do as well. Paint all the parts to be decorated with a thin solution of borax and water, the consistency of milk. Then fill the spaces with the ground niello, using a small spatula or flat wooden stick, mixing it with a little of the borax solution (**76, 4**). Drain off any surplus with a piece of blotting paper. Gently heat round the piece, keeping the flame off the niello, until the niello melts, and runs into the spaces prepared for it. If the flame is allowed to play directly on to the niello, it will burn it, causing bubbles and defects in the surface which cannot be removed. If there is insufficient niello in the spaces, cool the piece, reborax the areas which are not filled properly and spread another thin layer of niello so that it is flush with the metal. Then reheat the piece until the niello melts again. It is better to overfill rather than underfill the cavities, because the excess can be ground off. Let the piece cool slowly and when it is cold, rub the surface with a medium fine emery stick until all the raised metal is visible. Continue the polishing process with water of Ayr stone and water. You can also use pumice. Finish the polishing with tripoli and rouge (**76, 5**).

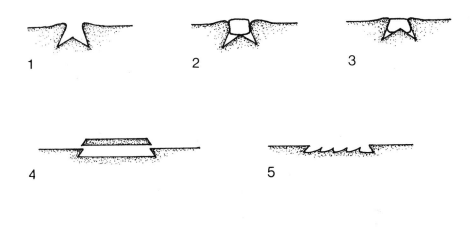

77 Sections of wire inlay
1 Double rooted line engraved with a bull sticker
2 Wire in place
3 Wire beaten into the engraved line
4 Undercut edge of base plate for inlay of bevelled plate
5 Surface of base plate raised with a graver
6 Simple inlay before undercutting

INLAY

Inlay is another development of engraving, consisting of carving out grooves or large areas in the metal surface and filling them with a different coloured metal. The grooves are filled with wire, but larger areas are inlaid with thin sheet. The inlay is hammered into place and held in position by the undercut edge of the surrounding metal. In order for this to be successful, the inlay metal must be softer than the one into which it is hammered. For example, silver may be inlaid into copper, 9ct or 18ct gold; 18ct soft gold wire and 22ct can be inlaid into silver. The metal base should be at least BMG 12, and can be thicker if you wish. When inlaying wire, always mark out the design on the metal first.

To cut the grooves to receive the wire, use a diamond graver, a bull sticker or a spit sticker. Each groove is made with two cuts of the graver. To do this, first tilt the tool to one side and cut along the line, then tilt it the other way as you cut again along the same line, thus making an undercut on both sides of the groove (**77, 1**). Keep the top width of the groove completely regular: if it is markedly wider in any part, the wire will tend to come out of the groove, and if it is much narrower, the wire will not go into it. The wire to be inlaid must be exactly the same width as the groove and slightly wider than it is deep (**77, 2**). Anneal the wire and insert one end into the groove. If the line to be inlaid has a beginning and an end, naturally start the wire inlay at one end, but if it is a continuous line, start where a join would be least conspicuous. Allow more than enough wire and cut it when the inlay is almost complete. Having inserted one end of the wire into the groove, ease the rest of the wire in. Using the chasing hammer, or a hammer with either a slightly rounded face or a ball face, beat carefully along the wire, so that it is driven under the undercut and spreads into the roots of the groove (**77, 3**). Keep the hammer blows on the wire: any blows which glance off the side of the inlay groove will damage the workpiece, making dents which are difficult to remove with a file. Having inlaid the wire into the groove, smooth over the lines with a planishing hammer or the rounded face of the chasing hammer. Then file and stone the whole surface smooth. An alternative to beating the wire in place with a hammer, is to use a matting tool. To make a matting tool, take a rod of thick steel, its diameter wider than the width of the inlay wire, and file a slight curve on one end. File and emery the curved end until it shines. Then use the matting tool as a punch to drive the wire under the undercut. The advantage of the matting tool as a punch is that you can position it accurately for each blow of the hammer.

The principle for inlaying areas of metal is the same, but it is best to start by piercing out the design to be inlaid from a sheet of thin metal for example BMG 4. Having cut out the piece, bevel its edge with a file, so that the bevel slopes outwards from the top surface (**77, 4**). Lay the inlay on the metal base and trace round its outline with a scriber. With a flat-edged graver carve out a recess slightly less deep than the thickness of the inlay metal, keeping the outline inside the traced outline, which will be fractionally larger than the inlay itself. Remember that the object is to achieve a perfect fit between the inlay and the base. Carve out the entire area to be filled by the inlay, using a chisel graver. Keep the surface as even as possible. The edge of the recess must be undercut with the bull sticker. To further secure the whole area of the inlay, raise a series of pointed burrs all over the floor of the recessed part, by digging the point of the square graver into the metal and raising the handle of the graver (**77, 5**). The spikes will become embedded in the lower surface of the inlay metal, acting like pegs when the inlay is beaten down on to them. When the negative and positive parts are ready to be joined, lay the base on a hard flat surface. Anneal the inlay and place it in position, then hammer it down evenly, using the flat face of the chasing hammer, or the planishing hammer. To protect the surface of the inlay metal, cover it with a piece of leather, or any other thick material which is not deeply textured. Alternatively, place a steel block over the inlay and hammer that. Not only will the surface be protected from hammer marks, but also the pressure on the inlay will be more widespread. Finally, file the piece flat, then stone and polish it.

There is another easier way of making the recess for the inlay metal which avoids carving it out. Take a sheet of the same metal as the background metal, and slightly thinner than the inlay sheet. Trace the outline of the inlay on to it and pierce out that outline, keeping inside the scribed line. Solder this sheet on to the base so that you have a recess with a perfectly flat floor. (77, 6). Undercut the edges with a bull sticker as before. Then anneal and hammer in the inlay as before.

There is another case for using solder for inlay work. It has already been said that for inlay work to be done, the inlay metal must be softer than the metal base into which it is hammered. The only way to inlay a harder metal into a softer surround is to solder it in place. To do this cover the floor of the recess with paillons of solder, borax them and heat them till the solder runs. Then reborax the area and place the inlay in position, heat the piece again till the solder runs again and fills the joins between the two metals. Use a solder which matches one or other of the metals so that it is not visible when the piece is finished.

11 Casting and fusing

Casting is the ancient method of producing or reproducing a piece of metalwork by making a mould of the original piece, and filling that mould with molten metal. The models can be made of metal or any other hard unyielding substance, of wax or of an organic material which burns away without leaving a large deposit of ashes. The process used to cast wax models is known as 'lost-wax' or '*cire perdue*'. There are several different methods of casting, which employ different materials for the moulds, and are suitable for different types of model. For occasional simple casting, cuttlefish bone or sand moulds are adequate. If you wish to cast work in large quantities it is worth while investing in some casting machinery. Casting machinery is sometimes available second hand from jewellers or dentists.

Cuttlefish bone casting

Casting small metal forms, such as little motifs, flowers or abstract shapes to use several times in a piece or pieces of jewellery, or reproducing simple rings, especially signet rings, can easily be done in cuttlefish

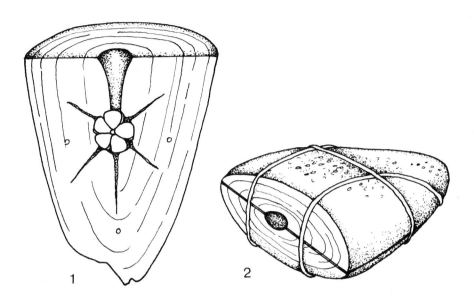

1   2

78 Cuttlefish casting
1 Model in place, with air channels,
pouring channel, and peg holes
2 Cuttlefish wired up ready for casting

bone. It is essential that the patterns are not undercut anywhere.

You will need a complete cuttlefish bone in good condition and a small crucible or a block of real, not composite, charcoal. Cut a straight edge along one end of the cuttlefish bone. Then cut the cuttlefish bone in half lengthways, using the saw or a sharp thin knife. If the cut is not a clean one, rub each edge perfectly flat on a piece of fine sandpaper card on a flat surface. Place three marker pegs, such as match sticks, in one side, allowing enough space between them for the pattern. Then press the two sides together to check that they fit perfectly.

Separate them again and push the pattern into one half between the pegs so that it projects above the surface of the cuttlefish (78, 1). Then press the other half firmly over it, so that a clean impression is made in both halves. Remove the pattern and carve a funnel shaped channel from the straight outside edge, to the impression left by the pattern. Then carve five or six channels radiating outwards from the pattern; these are holes for the air which is pushed out by the inrush of molten metal. Then tie the mould together with binding wire, lengthways, and widthways (78, 2). Fix it firmly upright on a piece of asbestos, with the pouring funnel at the top. If the asbestos is thick enough, hold the cuttlefish upright between four nails driven into the asbestos, alternatively support it with some heavy objects. Melt the gold or silver in a crucible or a block of charcoal. If you are using charcoal, make a small concavity about $\frac{1}{2}$in to $\frac{3}{4}$in from the edge of the block, then carve a shallow channel to the edge of the block. Have ready tongs, or a thick glove for your master hand to enable you to pick up the crucible or charcoal block when the metal is molten. Scraps of clean metal left over from previous work are useful for melting: several small pieces are easier to melt than a large lump. Borax and heat the metal until it melts into a shiny liquid globule which resembles mercury. Keep the flame directed on the metal all the time: any loss of heat will slow up the melting process; but it must not be overheated or allowed to boil. Any impurities which rise to the surface can be removed with a piece of flattened rod, such as a length of coat hanger wire.

When the metal is molten, pick up the block, keeping the flame directed on the metal and pour it quickly into the funnel of the cuttlefish mould. It is essential that the metal is completely molten at the moment of pouring. The casting will not be successful if the metal is not hot enough.

When the pattern has had time to cool, cut the binding wire, securing the cuttlefish, and let the pattern drop out on to a heat-resistant surface. It will keep its heat for some time, so beware of touching it with your fingers. Clean the piece in the pickle, and check it for accuracy. Even professional casters do not expect to achieve 100% accuracy every time. The chief difficulty is keeping the metal molten and pouring it at the same time.

To clean up the piece, first saw off the rods formed in the air channels and the pouring funnel. File off the casting surface where possible. Some parts difficult to file or polish may be cleaned with the burnishing tool. Filing sometimes reveals bubbles of air which have been trapped in the metal during the pouring. If they are very shallow, and the pattern allows it, file the metal down to remove them; if they are shallow, but the pattern would be spoilt by losing a layer of metal, fill them with solder, or drill a deeper hole and solder in a wire peg to fill the space. If the hole is deep and cannot be hidden, the only solution is to start again. For areas which cannot be filed smooth because they are inaccessible, use a brass brush on the polishing motor or the pendant drill to achieve a smoother surface than that left by the casting process.

Sand casting

Casting in sand is a method which can be used to produce larger pieces than is possible with cuttlefish bone, or it can be employed for the 'lost-wax' technique.

You need four or five pounds of fine sand, and some loam or clay. The sand must bind together well with some water and the clay. I have been unable to find casting sand sold commercially any longer, but the fine white or grey sand found on many beaches is suitable, and Hampstead, London sand is said to be excellent for the purpose! In addition you need a pair of casting flasks, some graphite and some fine brick dust in separate muslin bags. The casting flasks are two cast iron frames which fit together with pegs. These could be made with steel strips bolted together to form two open rectangles. In one side of each frame there is a semi-circular hole which forms a round hole when the frames are fitted together and through which the molten metal will be poured (**79, 1, 2**).

Place the casting flasks on a perfectly smooth flat board, the edges with the pouring holes resting on the board. Moisten the sand and loam thoroughly, and mix it well. Then pack it into the frames, beating it down with the mallet. Fill both frames with close packed sand till the sand is level with the frame edges. To level it off, place a flat board on the surface of each frame and turn them the right way up. Sprinkle both top surfaces with brick dust to prevent them sticking together. The moulds are now ready to receive the pattern, but the pattern must first be dusted with graphite to prevent sand from sticking to it. Embed the pattern in the sand of one of the frames in line with the pouring hole, at least an inch from the edge. The distance between the pouring hole and the pattern is important. If the distance is too small, there will not be sufficient weight of molten metal above the pattern to drive it into all the crevices of the mould, but if the distance is too great, relative to the area of the pattern, the metal will cool before it can fill the mould. When you are satisfied that the pattern is driven so firmly into the sand that it will leave a clean impression of its surface, dust the exposed surface of the pattern and the surrounding sand with the brick dust again. Place the other half of the frame over the pattern, so that it fits the lower half, then beat it with the mallet. Remove the top frame, blow away any loose sand and very carefully remove the pattern. Dust both halves of the impression with fine powdered charcoal, and press the pattern back into position to take a final impression. Remove

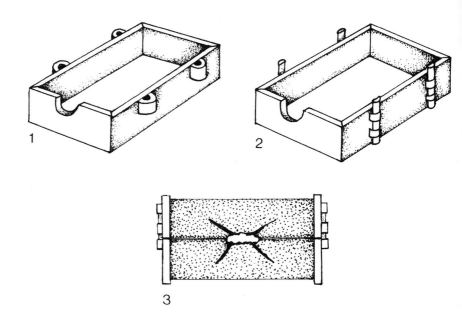

79 Casting flask
1 Bottom half
2 Upper half
3 Section through flask filled with sand, ready for casting

the pattern again and make the pouring channel and five or six air channels radiating from the pattern. If there are any projecting parts of the pattern, make an air channel from those points (**79, 3**).

Now assemble and dry the moulds in a hot place. This must be done thoroughly. When the sand is completely dry, keep the moulds hot whilst melting the metal in a crucible, then pour it in quickly. Clean up the castings as described for the cuttlefish castings. Castings from sand moulds may tend to be rougher than those done in cuttlefish, but the finish does depend considerably upon the quality of the sand and loam, and the care with which you make the impressions.

Lost-wax sand casting

Sand moulds may be used for the lost-wax method of casting. The lost-wax process produces the finest results of any casting process. The model is made in wax, invested in a material, in this case sand, which will take a negative impression of its form. When the sand is dry, it is heated to melt out the enclosed wax model, leaving a precise mould ready to receive the molten metal.

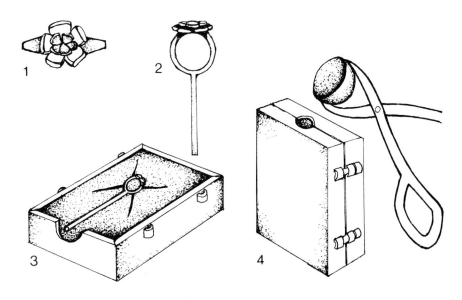

80 Lost-wax sand casting
1 Wax model of a flower ring
2 Wax model with sprue
3 The model placed in the sand filled frame
4 Pouring molten metal into the frame

For lost-wax sand casting, you need the sand and casting frames described for simple sand casting, and modelling wax. Modelling wax is available from some jewellers' suppliers, but dental wax from a dental supplier is ideal. It has a higher melting point than candle wax and can be combined with softer waxes which are useful for building up a surface texture. Learning to model the wax takes time. It is wise to keep to simple designs initially, building up patterns with the forms created by melting the wax and letting it drip, or rolling twig-like forms and melting the ends into beads.

To make a ring, wrap a wide strip of paper round a wooden dowel of the right finger size, bearing in mind that cast pieces are always marginally smaller than the original. Secure the paper at the edges with self-adhesive tape, so that it can be removed easily when the ring has been built round the dowel. The dental wax is available in thin sheets, so it is easy to cut out a strip for a simple ring, warm it slightly until it is malleable and bend it round a dowel to form a ring. To join it, pass a hot knife through both ends and weld them together. You can then decorate it by applying pieces of wax, or by cutting away parts with a warmed knife, or spatula made by flattening the end of a piece of wire (80, 1).

Having modelled the piece, attach to it three or four rods of wax which will form the sprue or pouring funnel, and the air channels. The sprue rod should be about $\frac{1}{8}$in diameter, terminating in an inverted cone which will form the funnel-shaped entrance to the pouring channel. Attach this to the largest area of wax, bearing in mind that when the metal sprue is sawn off the cast piece, it will leave a circle of plain metal, so chose an inconspicuous point (**80, 2**). The straight rods to form the air channels should be fixed to the wax model so that they radiate out from it.

Take the finest sand you can obtain and mix it with a little fine loam, then dry it thoroughly. Pound it with a pestle and mortar or grind it between two pieces of steel, such as the shaft of a large doming tool, and the steel block until it is a coarse powder. Then sift it through canvas or a fine mesh sieve into a bowl or a cup, and add enough water to make it a creamy liquid. Then leave it to settle. When the sand has settled, pour off the clear water, and with a soft paint brush made of camel or squirrel hair, paint the sand carefully over the whole wax model. To start with, very little will stick, but having applied one thin coat, let the model dry. When it is dry, apply another coat. Fill up all the crevices in the piece first, always allowing each coat to dry thoroughly before applying the next. Apply each coat evenly, using the paint brush in the same direction all the time if possible; avoid making holes or bubbles, by applying the sand too fast, too wet, or too thick.

Small wax pieces can be sand cast without the frames. Continue the process of painting sand on to the wax until it is at least one inch thick all over. Bind the mould round with binding wire and dry it carefully. Then use it in the same way as described for the framed sand mould. You must have a sprue but there is no need for air channels, because the air escapes through the sand. The results from small sand moulds are often better than those from frame moulds.

If you are sand-casting a larger wax model, when the model is covered with a crust of seven or eight carefully applied coats of sand which have all dried through, it is ready to be put in the casting frames. Partially fill one half of the frame with sand, and place the coated wax in it, so that the sprue is in line with the pouring hole. Press the sand in underneath it, so that the whole piece is well supported, then pack the sand well round it, until the whole frame is full of close-packed sand (**80, 3**). Lay the other frame on top of the lower one and fill that with well-packed sand too. Lay boards over the top and bottom of the frames and clamp them together firmly. Then place it in a warm place to dry. When the sand is dry, tip up the frame to allow any wax which may have melted to run out. Then place the frame in an oven or kiln, so that the remaining wax will run out – and be lost. Maintain the frame at a high temperature while you are melting the metal. Then support the frame on a heat proof surface and pour in the molten metal (**80, 4**). Keeping the mould hot whilst heating the metal is difficult to do alone. This operation is more easily completed by two people. When the frame has cooled, open the frame and break away the sand mould from the casting which can then be cleaned up.

Surface fusion and molten forms

These two techniques for treating gold or silver are included in this chapter because they both involve molten metal. They are equally relevant to Chapter 10 above.

The first method concerns the surface treatment of a work piece. If a sheet of metal is heated until it has begun to melt and is on the point of collapsing, and the flame is removed at the moment before it does actually collapse, a flowing molten effect remains on the metal. It requires split second timing to remove the flame before the piece collapses, though obviously, the thicker the metal, the longer the time margin. The surface of the metal suddenly changes from matt-red to a shiny shimmering effect, because it is actually melting. The results can be varied slightly by varying the intensity or the concentration of the flame on the metal so that some parts do melt and some do not, or some parts melt less than others. The effects will also vary according to whether the surface is boraxed all over or in parts.

Using the same method, additional pieces can be fused to the surface. Small pieces cut to an intended shape, or scraps of wire or off-cuts are arranged or scattered on the surface and boraxed well. When the metal is heated and begins to melt, the small pieces begin to melt too and become fused with the base. These techniques are not possible to control, but the random effects are often exciting and beautiful. Metal treated in this way can of course be incorporated in any piece of jewellery. For example you could set it with stones or pearls, use it for links in a chain or solder jump rings round part of its edge from which beads can be suspended and make it into a pendant or ear-rings.

To make forms which have an organic look similar to the surface effect achieved by the previous technique, you will need a bucket of cold water in addition to the blow torch, tongs, crucible, borax and metal to be melted. Place the metal in the crucible, borax it and heat it until it moves like mercury, then pick up the crucible with the tongs and maintain the heat to keep the metal molten up to the moment of pouring. Pour the metal quickly into the bucket from a height of at least two feet above the bucket. The effects achieved by this process vary considerably. The metal can take the most beautiful organic shapes, but it can also separate into globules like shot. The effects cannot be controlled and if the first results are disappointing, the only thing to do is to collect the metal, pickle it and start again. Sometimes shapes are formed which can be used alone, for example for the top of a ring, but several small pieces can be soldered together to form interesting shapes. If the edges are thin and brittle, they can sometimes be strengthened by playing a flame over them so that they melt and become thicker. It is essential that the metal is completely molten at the moment of pouring. Heating and reheating with a blow-pipe soon becomes exhausting, so bottled gas is extremely useful for the purpose.

Pouring molten metal from a height can obviously be hazardous. It is important to take great care that the crucible is well positioned over the bucket.

12 Design

It is impossible to teach design. All anyone can do is give suggestions and encouragement. Everyone has creative ability, which some find easier to express than others. Confidence plays an important part in the expression of an idea. Many people find it difficult to develop an idea far enough to execute it because their confidence to do so is in short supply. But it *is* worth persevering. Once started, one idea leads to another and confidence and ability grow.

Another hindrance to finding a starting point is the sheer number of possibilities offered by the wide variety of techniques and materials. If you are starting from the very beginning, it is advisable to make up the pieces described in this book, in order to get used to the tools and materials. Design and technical ability are closely linked, and before you know what can be done with a particular material, or what you can do, it is difficult to design a piece and make it. It is wise to accept that initially your technical ability is limited and to design within those limitations. However, I do not want to be the advocate of caution. There is a lot to be said for an adventurous approach.

One can look to innumerable sources for a starting point. Geometric forms appeal to some people, while others respond to organic or abstract shapes and all three are around us all the time. One way of starting is to take a shape which you like, say an oval, and build up a design using it repeatedly. It could be the basic motif for a linked necklace, composed of alternate domed silver ovals and pierced silver oval frames. You could include a larger oval frame, with one stone or several set inside the frame to hang as a pendant from the centre front of the necklace. Another possibility, using the same idea, is to set an oval stone in a plain silver setting such as the agate ring described in Chapter 8, and to decorate the sides of the ring with concentric ovals of applied gold wire, echoing the shape of the stone, or in a random pattern, overlapping each other, in contrast with the clean lines of the ring.

Nature has always been a source of ideas for artists in every area of design. Flowers, leaves, buds and many animals have been represented in different forms and materials by jewellers since the earliest jewellery made. There are many starting points to be found by looking at natural things. Flowers offer an inexhaustible source of shapes and colours. They can be represented in a realistic or stylized form. The petals of a flower could be pierced out of silver sheet and soldered to a solid base, such as a plain band ring, or they could be raised with doming punches in a sheet of metal, or they could be twisted up in wire. It is interesting to look at antique jewellery and to see the shapes and techniques used in previous eras, and this can also stimulate new ideas. There are many well illustrated books on the subject and several collections displayed in museums throughout the country. Having found a starting point, many ideas will develop from there.

If your interest lies entirely in the technical side of making jewellery, it is no sin to copy, and perhaps having made several pieces to other people's designs, you will feel you want to make up your own ideas. It is wise to decide on the design and to think through every stage of its construction before starting to make it. You can usually change or adapt your idea as you go along if improvements occur to you while constructing a piece. It is worthwhile giving the practical aspects of a piece a lot of thought; it is very frustrating to have a beautiful brooch which falls forward because the pin is in the wrong place, or a ring which scratches your fingers or tears your clothes because it has rough edges.

If a piece does not work, do not despair, everyone has setbacks, and if you can learn from your mistakes, they can even be useful. Making jewellery for your own enjoyment means you can make what you want and like.

Comparative gauges

Inch	Millimetre	Birmingham Metal Gauge (Shakespeare's) (BMG)	Standard Wire Gauge (SWG)	Approx. American wire or Brown & Sharpe (B & S)
·001	·025	—	50	—
·0012	·030	—	49	—
·0016	·041	—	48	—
·002	·051	—	47	—
·0024	·061	—	46	—
·0028	·071	—	45	—
·0032	·081	—	44	40
·0036	·091	—	43	39
·004	·102	—	42	38
·0044	·112	—	41	37
·0048	·122	—	40	—
·005	·127	—	—	36
·0052	·132	—	39	35
·006	·152	—	38	34
·0065	·165	—	—	—
·0068	·173	—	37	—
·007	·178	—	—	33

Inch	mm	BMG	SWG	B & S
·0076	·193	—	36	—
·008	·203	—	—	32
·0084	·213	—	35	—
·0085	·216	1	—	—
·009	·229	—	—	31
·0092	·234	—	34	—
·0095	·241	2	—	—
·010	·254	—	33	30
·0105	·267	3	—	—
·0108	·274	—	32	—
·011	·279	—	—	29
·0116	·295	—	31	—
·012	·305	4	—	—
·0124	·315	—	30	28
·013	·330	—	—	—
·0136	·345	—	29	—
·014	·356	5	—	27
·0148	·376	—	28	—
·015	·381	—	—	—
·016	·406	6	—	—
·0164	·417	—	27	26
·017	·432	—	—	—
·018	·457	—	26	25
·0185	·470	—	—	—
·019	·483	7	—	—
·020	·508	—	25	24
·0215	·546	8	—	—
·022	·559	—	24	23
·024	·610	9	23	—
·025	·635	—	—	22
·027	·686	—	—	—
·028	·711	10	22	21
·030	·762	—	—	—
·032	·813	11	21	20
·033	·838	—	—	—
·035	·889	12	—	—
·036	·914	—	20	19
·038	·965	13	—	—
·039	·991	—	—	—
·040	1·016	—	19	18
·042	1·067	—	—	—
·043	1·092	14	—	—
·046	1·168	—	—	17
·048	1·219	15	18	—
·049	1·244	—	—	—
·051	1·295	16	—	16
·055	1·397	17	—	—
·056	1·422	—	17	—
·058	1·473	—	—	15

Inch	mm	BMG	SWG	B & S
·059	1·499	18	—	—
·060	1·524	—	—	—
·062	1·575	19	—	—
·064	1·626	—	16	14
·065	1·651	20	—	—
·067	1·702	—	—	—
·069	1·753	21	—	—
·072	1·829	—	15	13
·073	1·854	22	—	—
·074	1·880	—	—	—
·077	1·956	23	—	—
·080	2·032	—	14	12
·082	2·083	24	—	—
·083	2·108	—	—	—
·086	2·184	—	—	—
·090	2·286	25	—	11
·091	2·311	—	—	—
·092	2·337	—	13	—
·095	2·413	—	—	—
·096	2·438	—	—	—
·100	2·540	26	—	—
·102	2·591	—	—	10
·104	2·642	—	12	—
·109	2·768	—	—	—
·110	2·794	—	—	—
·112	2·845	27	—	9
·116	2·946	—	11	—
·120	3·048	—	—	—
·121	3·073	—	—	—
·124	3·150	28	—	—
·128	3·251	—	10	8
·134	3·403	—	—	—
·136	3·454	29	—	—
·144	3·658	—	9	7
·148	3·759	—	—	—
·150	3·810	30	—	—
·160	4·064	—	8	6
·165	4·191	—	—	—
·166	4·216	31	—	—
·167	4·242	—	—	—
·176	4·470	—	7	—
·180	4·572	—	—	5
·182	4·623	32	—	—
·183	4·648	—	—	—
·192	4·877	—	6	—
·200	5·080	33	—	—
·201	5·105	—	—	—
·203	5·156	—	—	4
·212	5·385	—	5	—

Inch	mm	BMG	SWG	B & S
·213	5·410	—	—	—
·216	5·486	34	—	—
·220	5·588	—	—	—
·232	5·893	—	4	3
·238	6·045	35	—	—
·240	6·096	—	—	—
·249	6·325	—	—	—
·250	6·350	36	—	—
·252	6·404	—	3	—
·256	6·502	—	—	2
·259	6·578	—	—	—
·270	6·858	37	—	—
·276	7·010	—	2	—
·278	7·061	38	—	—
·284	7·214	—	—	—
·289	7·341	39	—	1
·300	7·620	40	1	—

Bibliography
List of suppliers
Index

Bibliography

BALL, Fred
Experimental Techniques in Enamelling Van Nostrand Reinhold

BRADFORD, Ernle
Four Centuries of European Jewellery Spring Books 1967

CHAMBERLAIN, Walter
Manual of Etching & Engraving Thames & Hudson 1973

CHOTE
Creative Casting Crown

EDWARDS
Lost Wax Casting of Jewellery Allen & Unwin

EVANS, Joan
A History of Jewellery 1100–1870 Faber, Rev. Ed. 1970

FALKINER, Richard
Investing in Antique Jewellery Corgi Books 1971

FLOWER, Margaret
Victorian Jewellery Cassell 1957

GERE, Charlotte
Victorian Jewellery Design William Kimber 1972

GERE, Charlotte
European & American Jewellery Heinemann 1975

GOODDEN, Robert and Philip Popham
Silversmithing O.U.P. Handbook

GREGORIETTI, Guido
Jewellery through the Ages Paul Hamlyn 1970

HOLLANDER, Henry
Plastics for Jewellery Pitmans 1974

JACK, Greta
Jewellery Making by the Lost Wax Process Van Nostrand Reinhold

ROSENBERG
Metal Enamelling Allen & Unwin

SCARFE, Herbert
Introducing Resin Craft Batsford 1973

SELWYN, A.
The Retail Jeweller's Handbook

SNOWMAN, Kenneth A.
The Art of Carl Fabergé Faber

SMITH, G. F. Herbert (Revised by F. C. Phillips)
Gemstones Chapman Hall 1972

SMITH, Keith
Practical Silversmithing & Jewellery Studio Vista 1975

UNTRACHT, Oppi
Metalwork Techniques for Craftsmen Robert Hale 1974

WEBSTER, Robert
Gemmologist's Compendium N.A.G. Press Ltd 1970

WILSON, H.
Silverwork & Jewellery Pitman 1966

ZECHLIN, Katharina
Creative Enamelling & Jewellery Making Oaktree Press 1966

Craftwork in Plastic (Polyester Resins) Search Press 1972

List of suppliers

1. *Precious Metals and Findings*

J. Blundell and Sons Ltd
199 Wardour Street
London W1

Johnson Matthey & Co Ltd
78 Hatton Garden   +   Victoria Street
London EC1   Birmingham 1

                          +   75–79 Eyre Street
                              Sheffield

D. Pennellier & Co Ltd
28 Hatton Garden
London EC1

Sheffield Smelting Co Ltd +   132 St John Street
St Pauls Square   London EC1
Charlotte Street
Birmingham 13   +   Royds Mill Street
                              Sheffield

2. *Base Metals*

Aluminium Goods Ltd
Rocky Lane
Birmingham 7

Aluminium Wire and Cable Co Ltd
Great Western Buildings   +   Glen House
6 Livery Street   Stag Place
Birmingham 3   London SW1

Ash & Lacey Ltd
Meriden Street
Birmingham 5

Aston Aluminium Warehouse Co Ltd
Fenthan Road
Aston
Birmingham

Blackburns Ltd
Drayton House
Gordon Street
London WC1

Brockside Metal Co Ltd
Astra Works
Honeypot Lane
Stanmore
Middlesex

Brown Bros Ltd
Downs Road
London E5

Clay Bros & Co
6b Spring Bridge Road
London W5

Deutch & Brenner Ltd
Alliance Works
Barford Street
Birmingham 18

B. Grundy & Co Ltd
Shelford Place
London N16

A. D. Keeling & Co Ltd
Warstone Metal Works
Hall Street
Birmingham 18

Kemp & Son Ltd
Tenby Street North
Birmingham 1

London Metal Warehouse Ltd
16a Prospect Row   +   431 Edgware Road
Birmingham   London W2

                          +   14 Prudhoe Street
                              Newcastle upon Tyne

                          +   Brinksway Bank Mill
                              Stockport

J. F. Ratcliff (Metals) Ltd
New Summer Street
Birmingham 19

H. Rollett & Co Ltd
32/36 Rosebery Avenue
London EC1

William Rowland Ltd
9 Meadow Street
Sheffield 3

T. W. Senier & Co Ltd
115 St John Street
London EC1

J. Smith & Sons Ltd
50 St Johns Square
Clerkenwell
London EC1

Willbraham & Smith Ltd
260 Grays Inn Road
London WC1

3. *Precious and Semi-Precious Stones*

Gemrocks Ltd
7 Brunswick Centre
London WC1

C. Calipé
44 Poland Street
London W1

Beach
41 Church Street
Twickenham
Middlesex

King Lapidary
1 Albemarle Way
London EC1

4. *Jewellers' Tools*

Charles Cooper Ltd
92–93 Hatton Garden
London EC1

E. Gray & Sons Ltd
12 Clerkenwell Green
London EC1

Frank Pike
58g Hatton Garden
London EC1

A. J. Plunkett & Co Ltd
88 Camberwell Road
London SE5

C. V. Salvo Ltd
88 Hatton Garden
London EC1

Thomas Sutton (Birmingham) Ltd
166 Warstone Lane
Birmingham 18

S. Tyzack & Son Ltd
341 Old Street
London EC1

George Panton & Sons
Buchanan Street
Glasgow

5. *Dental Suppliers*

Claudius Ash Sons & Co Ltd
26 Broadwick Street
London W1

6. *Electro Platers and Finishers*

F. P. Richards
7 Poland Street
London W1   (+many others)

7. *Castings*

M. and S. Rinberg & Co Ltd
6 St Cross Street
London EC1

8. *Etching and Engraving Suppliers*

Hunter Penrose Littlejohn Ltd
7 Spa Road
London SE16

9. *Polyster Resins*

Strand Glass
109 High Street
Brentford
Middlesex

10. *Perspex*

R. Denny & Co Ltd
13–15 Netherwood Road
London W14   (+many others)

11. *Modelling Equipment*

Tiranti
21 Goudge Place
London W1

Additional Sources of Supply

Alcob Metals Ltd
St Marks Road
London W11

Index